Contents

Contents

The Essence of Marketing Research

Peter M. Chisnall

Prentice Hall

New York   London   Toronto   Sydney   Tokyo   Singapore

First published 1991 by
Prentice Hall Europe Ltd
Campus 400, Maylands Avenue, Hemel Hempstead
Hertfordshire HP2 7EZ
A division of
Simon & Schuster International Group

Typeset in 10/12 pt Palatino
by Keyset Composition, Colchester, Essex

Transferred to digital print on demand 2002

Printed and bound by Antony Rowe Ltd, Eastbourne

Library of Congress Cataloging-in-Publication Data

Chisnall, Peter M.
    The essence of marketing research / Peter M. Chisnall.
        p.   cm. — (The Essence of management series)
    Includes bibliographical references and index.
    ISBN 0-13-284829-5 *10 0614 5968*
    1. Marketing research.   I. Title.   II. Series.
HF5415.2.C47   1991
658.8'3 — dc20   90-20454
                                                           CIP

British Library Cataloguing in Publication Data

Chisnall, Peter M. (Peter Michael)
The essence of marketing research.
1. Marketing. Research
I. Title   II. Series
658.83

ISBN 0-13-284829-5

Preface

Marketing research has a specific function: to aid effective planning and decision making in markets. These may be of many kinds and involve consumer, industrial, commercial and institutional activities.

In my well-established (and lengthier) book on marketing research (McGraw-Hill, 3rd edition, 1986), I proposed that marketing research should be viewed as a form of applied research which, while imposing on its practitioners the rigours and discipline of scientific enquiry, has a pragmatic purpose. Hence, an objective posture and systematic methods of enquiry are vital constituents of marketing research.

This text aims to give concise yet comprehensive information about the nature, scope, tools and techniques of marketing research. Deliberately, academic references are minimal; the focus has followed the title of this publishing series, namely to concentrate on the essence of this versatile and indispensable approach to the development of successful marketing strategies. To illustrate some of the many applications of marketing research I have, through the goodwill of the Market Research Society and the Managing Editor of *Survey*, Ms Phyllis Vangelder, and with the ready cooperation of the authors, included some short case histories. I am very grateful for their generous and professional help. I should also thank the executives of one of the leading North West research companies who kindly provided the case history entitled *Evaluating Direct Selling Effectiveness*.

This book is distilled in part from my larger academic text, and I am grateful to McGraw-Hill for their pleasant cooperation and willing agreement.

I must also thank the following leading market survey organizations: IPA (JICNARS), CACI International, Research International (RBL) and Research Services Ltd ('Sagacity') which have kindly allowed me to reproduce details of some of their services. In addition, the extracts from the *Standard Industrial Classification* (Revised 1980) are given by permission of the Controller of Her Majesty's Stationery Office. I also acknowledge with pleasure the friendly and professional help of my publishers with whom I have earlier collaborated in the production of *Strategic Industrial Marketing*, and last, but certainly not least, my thanks are given to Mrs Mary Mason of Dublin Business School for her secretarial expertise in producing, at short notice, a typescript of high standard.

1

Introduction

The successful development of a business calls for entrepreneurial flair and good organizing ability. Without entrepreneurial energy and leadership, businesses are unlikely to prosper, particularly in the highly competitive environment which typifies most industries today. The function of marketing is to assume the role and responsibilities of the entrepreneur whose traditional role has been to interpret market requirements and to relate these to the resources which are currently available, or which it may be feasible to acquire within the medium and long term.

These tasks are common to all organizations, whether they are primarily motivated by profits generated through competitive activities, or they are active in providing, for example, health, social or educational services in the public sector.

In all these diverse activities, customer or client orientation should be the motivating force; the precept, as Adam Smith observed over two hundred years ago, is simple but the practice is frequently complex. This sequential approach is outlined in Figure 1.1.

Vital inputs to business success

When businesses were small and their customers few, specialized functions of management were largely unnecessary. The sturdy founders of these early enterprises knew their customers well and had almost daily contact with them. But as businesses grew bigger and markets expanded geographically as well as in total sales, distinct functions of management evolved. In modern business practice the specialized functions of management are interdependent; expertise

1

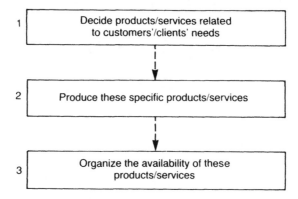

Figure 1.1 Sequential approach to principal tasks of management

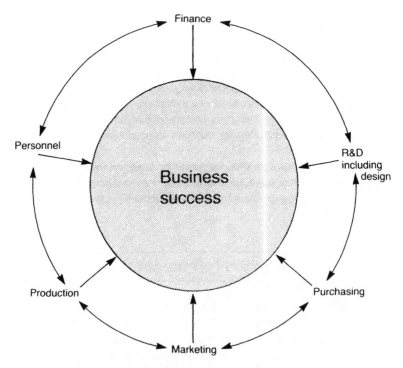

Figure 1.2 Vital inputs to business success

from production, purchasing, personnel, research and development (R and D) (including design) and finance contribute to business success. These vital marginal inputs and relationships are shown in Figure 1.2.

Marketing expertise is a necessary but not sufficient condition for success in competitive environments. Linkages between management specialisms should be actively forged; marketing management should make sure that everyone in their company is aware of the nature of their markets, for example customers' needs and competitors' activities, so that a real team effort takes place through every department of the firm.

Information about markets, i.e. market research data, should be discussed with designers, production engineers, purchasing officers and so on. Marketing research should not be hoarded and used merely by marketing departments; full value should be extracted from such important data so that, for example, product improvements and innovations can be planned to coincide with the needs of specific market segments.

Marketing: a business philosophy and a management function

Marketing has two important aspects: it is a basic philosophy of business which is inspired by the wish to serve customers well so that they will buy (and continue to buy) the goods and services offered to them by individuals and competing suppliers. Customer orientation is the motivating force behind such businesses; no customers: no business.

Marketing is also a specialized function of management and has a key role in building profitable businesses. It has already been seen that in small businesses the owner or general manager will undertake many responsibilities, including those of marketing management, but as companies grow larger marketing becomes more sophisticated and specially trained management is necessary.

Critical facets of marketing management

Three special areas of activity are involved in successful marketing management:

1. Analysis.
2. Planning.
3. Control.

In real life these functions overlap, but they are distinguished here for purposes of discussion.

Analysis
This is a particularly critical responsibility of marketing management: it relates to finding out about the markets in which a company operates at present or which it is planning to enter. Through systematic market research present and emergent needs will be identified, analysed and evaluated. Both quantitative and qualitative assessments should be involved so that a comprehensive view can be taken of market behaviour and opportunities.

Planning
Planing follows logically from the analytical approach, which is the hallmark of professional marketing. From the data derived from the marketing research process, management should be in a position to select markets suitable for exploitation; products and services designed to satisfy the identified needs of specific markets should then be developed – as discussed earlier under the heading 'Vital inputs to business success'.

Apart from developing new products and services, existing ones can be improved as the result of information gathered through objective market enquiries. Many companies are alert to the need to improve and update their products from time to time. Fundamental changes in technology also underly the urgency of keeping closely in touch with market behaviour; technological change and planned obsolescence affect not only consumer products but, increasingly, industrial demand. New competitors may also enter markets and challenge the long-held supremacy of traditional suppliers.

In general, there is no shortage of production capacity in modern industrialized economies; there is certainly a dearth of really talented marketing skills, particularly in organizational supplies (this will be further discussed later). Strategic planning sets the direction and pace of a business and maps the route it should take for its long-term success.

Control
Control – the third area of successful marketing – is vital to the productivity of a business or, indeed, any type of organization. Standards of performance (for example cost/sales ratios, market share, territory quotas, product performance, etc.) need to be set and closely monitored.

Cost effectiveness measures the performance and progress of a business in many ways. For example, distribution as well as production needs to be carefully investigated for its relative contribution to overall success. Continuous monitoring of sources of supply of essential raw materials and components ensures that the final products are produced to consistently high standards. Marketing management, as previously mentioned, should recognize that success in markets depends substantially on total commitment to management control throughout the business and an awareness of the need for specialists in marketing, production, design, finance, purchasing, personnel, etc. to work creatively together to achieve the objectives of the organization to which they all belong.

SUMMARY

Business success is built up from identifying and serving the needs of customers efficiently. Marketing management has three distinct aspects: analysis, planning and control. Market research is the crucial analytical approach and provides management with vital strategic and tactical information for decision making.

2

Marketing research

Nature of marketing research

Marketing research is concerned with the systematic and objective collection, analysis and evaluation of information about specific aspects of marketing problems in order to help management make effective decisions. Marketing research is not an end in itself; it is a means to an end – the improvement of decision making. These decisions may affect the nature and range of products, pricing policy, distribution strategy, promotional activities and so on; in fact, virtually every aspect of serving customers or clients well – from the idea stage onwards.

The complexity of modern business decisions calls for reliable knowledge of diverse markets. Managerial experience and judgement are, or course, important ingredients of decision making, but they should be reinforced and expanded by objective data from systematic field investigations.

Perhaps the term 'marketing research' (or 'market research' – a popular synonym) has discouraged wider adoption of this management technique. To commercial management it may, perhaps, have overtones of pure academic research, such as that conducted in a research laboratory under controlled conditions, divorced from 'reality' and perceived to be of little direct help in making difficult business decisions. However, this is not so, for marketing research, while adopting a scientific approach and using some of the well-tested methodologies of scientific investigations, is nearer to the function of field intelligence than of the research laboratory. Indeed, it would be more appropriate to consider marketing research as a form of applied research which, while imposing on its practitioners the rigours and discipline of scientific enquiry, has a pragmatic purpose. Without this scientific orientation, marketing research would have little validity; it would degenerate into subjective assessments of market behaviour.

Liberal roots of marketing research

Marketing research has borrowed liberally from other disciplines; this is not surprising, as research methodologies and techniques have application over many fields of study. Like other emerging disciplines, marketing research theory has been developed by creative adaptation rather than blind adoption. For example, from statistics marketing research has taken the theory of sampling which is fundamental to the whole process of objective enquiry; from economics have been borrowed descriptive analyses of the structure of industries, business trends and general economic data; psychology, sociology and cultural anthropology have contributed concepts of human behaviour which have enriched earlier economic projections of buying behaviour. Concepts such as social class structure, group behaviour, social trends and cultural influences leading to customs, conventions and taboos have been assimilated by marketing researchers. This process of selective borrowing, adaptation and synthesis has enabled marketing research to make a unique contribution to management decision making: it should be the core element of marketing strategy.

Importance of relevant data

Managers should not expect too much from marketing research; objective data need skilful interpretation. It is feasible for the data to be of exceptional quality but for the wrong decisions to be taken, perhaps because the data have been misinterpreted and/or wrong prognoses have been made. The fact that techniques such as marketing research reduce the element of risk in management decisions does not absolve managers from exercising skill, judgement and initiative. The interpretation of market research data may give rise to different opinions which may be hotly argued (this aspect will be discussed more fully later).

Often, there is no shortage of information in organizations; the trouble is that it is frequently the wrong kind of information – excessive, irrelevant, incompatible and outdated. Relatively simple but up to date market information is more useful to management than sophisticated analyses which have lost most of their value because of excessive delay in collection and presentation. Discrimination should be exercised in the selection of data; sheer abundance merely leads to computerized confusion. Management information should not be gathered indiscriminately or as a 'play-safe' strategy; before seeking information marketing management should discipline their search by defining with care the nature of the problem facing them. Too frequently, managers appear to be trying to solve problems which they have not identified accurately or adequately.

The dynamic nature of many markets underlines the need for managers to keep their information up to date. In a rapidly changing environment, it is folly to rely on data gathered years ago; regular monitoring of trends is essential – this enables significant developments to be spotted in time to take vital decisions.

Categories of information needs

Good information is the raw material needed by management in deciding a company's policy and day-to-day operations. Information for marketing decision making may be broadly classified as (i) strategic; (ii) tactical and (iii) 'data bank'. The first type refers to information needed for strategic decisions, for example whether to enter a specific overseas market or to diversify into new markets; the second type relates to information for tactical decisions, such as the planning of sales territories; the third type provides essential background knowledge about, for example, competitors' activities, market trends, VAT requirements and so on. Such information needs regular updating.

In practice, of course, these categories of information tend to become blurred and companies often require a 'mix' of information.

Two-way flow of marketing information
Marketing management information has a two-way flow: from the organization to the environment (that is, the market) and from the environment to the organization; the principle of feedback is an essential element (see Figure 2.1). Successful companies keep closely in touch with their customers and monitor carefully competitors'

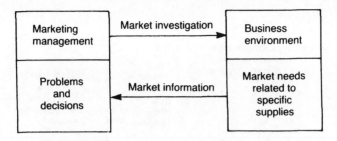

Figure 2.1 Two-way flow of marketing information

activities. Over time valuable background knowledge is built up (the 'data bank' already mentioned), and management may well have sufficient information at their fingertips to allow them to make certain market decisions without further enquiry. Often, however, the data bank, while impressive, cannot fully satisfy their information needs and specific research is necessary (see Chapter 7 for further discussion of this vital topic).

Preliminary evaluation
In order, therefore, to make decisions that are likely to lead to successful business, marketers need to:

(i) assess the extent of their existing knowledge about specific markets;

(ii) relate this store of knowledge to the types of decisions they have to make;

(iii) specify the nature of additional information they would need before particular decisions could be made within an acceptable degree of risk (see Figure 2.2).

This systematic approach, as noted earlier, starts with defining as closely as possible the projected target market. For example, the UK domestic furniture market has three major segments catering for specific living needs: bedroom furniture, kitchen furniture and living/dining-room furniture. Within these sectors, further product differentiations occur, such as upholstered furniture, wooden furniture, self-assembly furniture and so on. Virtually every market has special characteristics affecting demand both home and overseas.

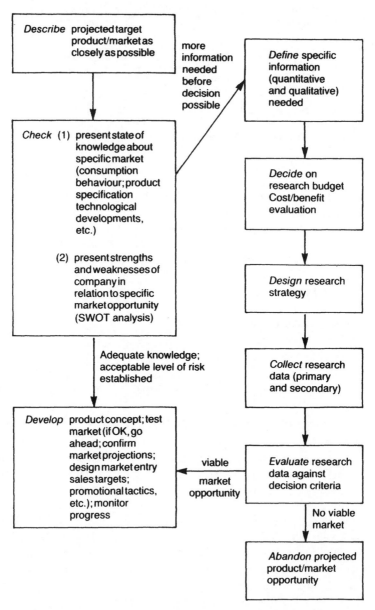

Figure 2.2 Outline scheme of marketing research related to product/market strategy

Main divisions of marketing research

Marketing research can cover many aspects involved in the marketing of goods and services. It is useful to differentiate broad divisions of these responsibilities, although, of course, these tend to be rather arbitrary and it would be unrealistic and, indeed, naïve to expect water-tight compartments (see Figure 2.3).

Product research
Product research is concerned with the design, development and testing of new products, the improvement of existing products and the forecasting of likely trends in consumers' preferences related to styling, product performance, quality of materials and so on. Included in this evaluation will be pricing studies, pack acceptability and product line acceptability.

Customer research
Customer research covers investigation into buyer-behaviour – studying the social, economic, cultural and psychological influences affecting purchase decisions, whether these are taken at the consumer level, the trends distribution level or in the industrial field (see Figure 2.4 for outline model of complex buying influences).

The complexity of modern patterns of consumption demands sophisticated understanding; explanations based solely on economic theory are clearly inadequate. The other social sciences – sociology, anthropology and psychology – can provide extra valuable knowledge

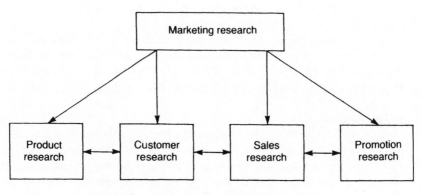

Figure 2.3 Main divisions of marketing research

11

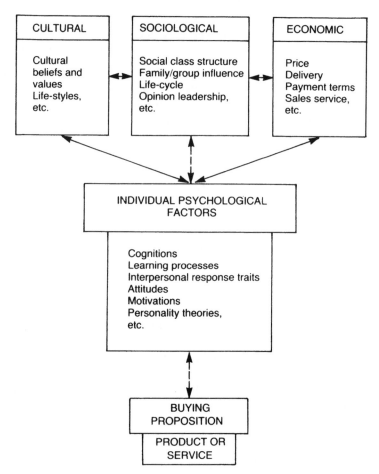

Figure 2.4   The complex pattern of buying influences

of buying behaviour, so research should be comprehensive and involve many facets. As observed already, it is also important to collect both qualitative and quantitative data. (For extended discussion refer to *Marketing: A Behavioural Analysis*, Peter M. Chisnall, and Chapter 4.)

Sales research

Sales research involves a thorough examination of the selling activities of a company, usually by sales outlets, territories, agencies and so on. Present sales trends should be checked and the comparative position related to competitors must be evaluated. Alternative methods of distribution may be examined and feasibility studies conducted.

Promotion research

Promotion research is concerned with testing and evaluating the effectiveness of the various methods used in promoting a company's products or services. These activities include exhibitions, public relation campaigns, merchandising, consumer and trade advertising and so on. In overseas markets, the availability of specific mass media should be carefully researched; the pattern of the mass media in the UK is by no means the same as in other countries.

Alternative and complementary forms of product promotion can be researched during the course of trade and consumer surveys. Where a company operates in more than one market, separate promotional policies will be drawn up as the result of information collected through marketing research in specialized market sectors.

This necessarily brief account of the various ways in which marketing research can give practical help in developing effective marketing strategies and tactics indicates the versatility of this management information tool. However, like all tools, it needs to be used with skill and with a firm understanding not only of its capabilities but also of its limitations. In the next chapter, discussion will focus on the stages of marketing research and the methodologies involved.

SUMMARY

Marketing research has sprung from liberal roots – social research. Its theoretical approach and methodologies have been borrowed from probability statistics, descriptive economics, psychology, sociology and cultural anthropology. This process of selective borrowing, adaptation and synthesis has given marketing research a distinctive value and character.

Data collection should be disciplined; information needs are: strategic, tactical and data bank (or a blend of all). Information flows two ways: from the firm to the environment, and vice versa. Organizations should assess their present state of knowledge about specific problems before committing themselves to extended research.

Marketing research covers four main areas: product, customer, sales, promotion. Buying is a complex process involving sophisticated appreciation of the many factors influencing demand. Some of these influences may not always be readily identifiable, but that does not mean that they should be ignored.

3

Sequential stages of marketing research

Value of systematic approach

The approach to any task is more effective if it is systematically organized: market research is no exception to this golden rule.

Five logical steps can be identified in the survey process: these apply irrespective of the nature of the market – consumer, industrial or public service (see Figure 3.1). The various stages indicated and described later are common to research activities of many kinds. A disciplined approach and attention to detail will ensure that the resultant data will be of high quality and that the final report gives real insight into market behaviour. These five stages of the research programme will now be discussed in some detail.

Stage 1: research brief
This diagnostic stage will involve initial discussions between clients and researchers in order to obtain a clear indication of the marketing problems. The following are typical questions to be covered during the briefing process.

Industry background and nature of products made by company

What industry/industries does the company operate in, and what products/services are offered by company?

Who buys these products?

Sequential stages of marketing research

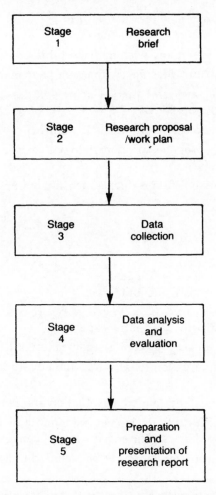

Figure 3.1 Five sequential stages of marketing research programme

What market share or shares are held by company and its competitors?

What particular skills or other advantages does the company have?

What are the general marketing objectives and strategies of the company?

Proposed topic of market investigation

What is the specific product/service on which research should focus?

Is this an entirely new product/service
(a) to the company? (b) to the market?

Why does the company wish to market this product?

How and to whom does the company hope to market this product?

What volume sales and market share for this product does the company hope to achieve?

What specific product attributes are planned?

How does this proposed product fit in with existing production and marketing skills?

What time horizons for product launch and market development are envisaged?

Extent of market research activities

Is the market to be investigated:
(a) home? (b) export? (c) both?

If export markets are to be surveyed, are there particular countries of which the company has special experience?

What is the overseas marketing organization of the company?

Does the company plan to introduce the new product in the home market first?

Does the brief extend to media evaluation and recommendations?

Does the brief include design recommendations for the proposed new product, or have design specifications been researched already?

Are pricing recommendations to be included in the survey?

The first stage is critical, because it will decide the nature and direction of the entire research activities. This involves defining precisely the marketing problem which is to be the focus of the survey. Before this is feasible exploratory enquiries may be necessary; this will give researchers the opportunity of gaining valuable insight into an organization and its market problems. Both management and researchers should work closely together in this crucial task of developing survey objectives. As indicated in Chapter 2, it is extremely important to define clearly the actual population to be surveyed.

The term 'population' is used in the statistical sense and refers to the subject under survey, which might be an industry, a section of the distributive trades, a consumer market such as toiletries or, perhaps, might refer to the expenditure patterns and preferences of certain age-groups in the UK. It is essential to define, for example, geographical areas so that there can be no misunderstanding about territorial coverage. Demographic definitions should also be precise: what, for instance, is meant by 'teenagers'; these are often measured in differing age spans. Industries can be usefully described by referring to the official *Standard Industrial Classification* (discussed later). In some cases, surveys have lost much of their value because of carelessness in describing adequately the population covered by the enquiries, so attention to well-devised definitions of survey populations is strongly recommended.

Unless the briefing given to the researchers is thorough – and an unbiased account of the firm and its problems is given by management – the resultant research objectives may be irrelevant and even counter-productive. If the research is to be undertaken by outside specialists it is crucial for them to be given the opportunity to familiarize themselves with the organization and its products or services. The researcher should indicate the limitations of specific survey methodologies; both parties should agree on the degree of accuracy required, the date by which the report is to be submitted and the appropriate costs involved. (These aspects of the research will be covered in the next phase of the research process.)

Stage 2: research proposal
The information gathered in stage one will be studied by researchers who will then submit a detailed research proposal to clients for approval. This should be evaluated for its overall logic and understanding of the problem(s) in questions. The proposal is likely to contain the following items, which should be carefully checked by clients.

Clear statement of nature of marketing problem(s) to be investigated.

Principal contributory factors and constraints related to this problem (see Figure 3.2).

Precise definition of product/service which is to be investigated.

Precise definition of survey population to be sampled.

Major areas of measurement, e.g. consumption, beliefs about products, expectations, attitudes, motivations, classifications of buyers (present and prospective), process of decision making, frequency of purchase, media exposure, etc. Industry concentration,

17

Beliefs — *what people believe they hold to be facts:*
but not all facts are beliefs

Consumption
Attitudes
Motivations
Life-styles
Socio-cultural aspects
Demographic trends
Industry concentration
Economic trends
Technological developments
Competitive activities

Figure 3.2 Major facets of measurement

economic trends, technological developments, will also be important in industrial marketing research (see Figure 3.2).

Methodology to be adopted (types of data, method of sampling, research instruments, etc.).

Degree of accuracy of survey findings.

Costs and time involved in survey.

Conditions applying to research survey.

Experience of researchers in conducting specific kinds of research.

An effective research design is the foundation of the entire research process and management clients should discuss with marketing researchers the proposed methods of investigation, the nature and extent of their coverage and so on. Eventually, this proposal should be agreed in detail before authorization is given to proceed with the fieldwork. Like all experts, marketing researchers have highly developed skills of which management should take full advantage; this means being prepared to spend time with the researchers *before* the investigations are put in hand and acquiring a firm grasp of the work that is going to be undertaken.

Stage 3: data collection
Data for marketing research can be obtained by several methods; the research proposal will have submitted a general outline of the

methodology. No research method is without bias; it is the task of professional researchers to eliminate, as far as possible, the intrusiveness of bias in surveys. Two main types of data are classified as: (a) primary data; (b) secondary data. Primary data relate to information collected for the first time, unique to that particular investigation and can be collected by either one or a blend of: (a) observation; (b) experimentation; (c) questionnaires. While the basic method of questionnaires is generally popular for collecting primary data the two other methods may be used, but their applications are limited mostly to fast-moving, consumer product markets. The use of more than one method of collecting survey data helps to offset the biases which, inevitably, are associated with specific techniques such as personal interviewing. (This point will be further examined in the next chapter.)

Secondary data refer to existing information which is useful for a specific survey. (Refer to Appendix A.) This type of data may be available (a) internally; (b) externally. Secondary data research, also known as desk research, should always be undertaken before doing any field survey. It is economical, comparatively speedy and can be undertaken with complete confidentiality. In some cases, desk research may result in adequate knowledge for particular decisions.

Companies should check their internal routine records carefully to see whether marketing information could be gleaned at low cost. With a little ingenuity, significant marketing data may be extracted, for example, from accounting records. Even today, many companies fail to utilize fully the information about customers and their patterns of buying which may be culled from records of transactions; for example, from invoices.

External secondary data are available from diverse sources: government reports, official statistics, trade associations, and so on. (Consult the Central Statistical Office for relevant sources of official data.) The acquisition of secondary data depends on the following four factors: availability, relevance, accuracy and cost. Each factor should be carefully assessed in order to ensure that relevant, valid and cost-effective information is obtained in specific enquiries.

Stage 4: data analysis and evaluation
The tasks of data processing and evaluation are discussed in Chapter 7.

Stage 5: preparation and presentation of research report
The various responsibilities of this final stage of the research process are also given in Chapter 7.

Sampling methodology

Sampling methodology is the foundation of the research design: it deserves special attention. A sample is a microcosm of the population from which it is drawn; it can only be accepted as accurate within certain limits. Samples must be representative so that valid conclusions about their population can be inferred. However, a sample cannot reflect a perfect image of the population from which it is drawn; some degree of distortion will, unfortunately, occur, but this can largely be controlled through applying sound principles of sampling. Values in population are known are parameters; those in samples are termed statistics (see Figure 3.3).

In practice, a census is rare in commercial research except where the population under survey is quite small and easily located, as may happen in some specialized industrial research. Most censuses are directed by governments to provide vital information on, for example, trends in population and trade and industry. They are expensive, relatively slow and comparatively rare.

Sampling is widely used in market research and its methodologies were pioneered many years ago by social investigators such as Bowley who undertook notable enquiries into the conditions of the working class in Reading. His disciplined approach strongly influenced the methodology of social surveys, which became more systematic in the use of sampling technologies. Sampling theory is based on the relationships between a population (not necessarily, as stated already, a human population – the term is used in its statistical sense) and the samples drawn from it. Probability theory allows certain conclusions to be drawn about a specific population and the samples taken from it.

As noted, sampling has a key role to play in systematic, objective market surveying. It has many attractions: it saves money, time and labour; frequently, it enables data of high quality to be collected which

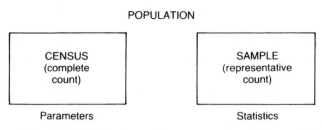

Figure 3.3 Relationship of population parameters and sample statistics

would be outside the feasibility of a census. The overall cost of samples is lower than a census or complete investigation, but the cost per unit of study may be higher because of the need to employ skilled interviewers, administrative costs incurred in sample design, etc. A big advantage of sample surveys over censuses is that of availability of the eventual report. Censuses take many years to prepare for publication, whereas survey reports can be published in a few months.

There are two main types of sample:

(a) random – 'probability': this occurs where each element of a population from which the sample is drawn has a known (and non-zero) chance of being selected. For example, if a sample of 250 people is to be chosen at random from a defined population of 25,000, each member of that population will have one chance in 100 of being selected in the sampling process. Probability sampling is widely used by research bodies because of its sound theoretical basis. It is the only completely objective method of sampling populations and is used almost exclusively by the UK Government Social Survey and by the American Bureau of the Census.

(b) quota – 'non-probability': also known as judgement or purposive; this is a type of stratifed sampling in which selection of sampling units within specified strata (for example, age, sex, socio-economic group) is done by interviewers on a non-random basis, controlled to some extent by quotas allocated to the different strata. Hence, non-probability sampling is prone to interviewer bias, that is, the tendency for even experienced interviewers to select respondents subjectively. The data resulting from this type of sampling are, therefore, generally less reliable than those derived from random sampling where rigorous statistical tests can be applied. Although lacking rigorous statistical acceptability quota sampling is relatively speedy, economic and administratively simple. Because specifically nominated informants do not have to be interviewed and no expensive call-backs are involved, the flexibility of this method has made it attractive to market researchers.

Sampling frame

However, while random sampling is a statistically sounder methodology than quota or non-probability sampling, it has certain drawbacks. In order to use it, a *sampling frame* (a list) of the population under survey is necessary. Few adequate lists exist in commercial practice and it is usually expensive to generate them. Official lists, such as the Register of Electors, quickly become outdated.

Existing sampling frames should be carefully checked for their adequacy, completeness, lack of duplicated entries and suitability for specific research projects. The time taken to complete surveys is extended and costs are thus increased, because of the likelihood that randomly selected informants may be widely scattered. One of the chief practical disadvantages is the need to make 'call-backs', so as to interview randomly selected informants. Standard practice is for interviewers to make up to three calls before abandoning the prospect of an interview. It can readily be seen that considerable travel might be involved, with inevitable delays and costs. Some system of substitution of the originally selected informant is often used in order to preserve the size of the sample; but this does not entirely reduce the risk of bias.

Random or probability sampling should be applied extremely carefully in industrial market investigations, particularly where industries are dominated by a few large companies. If one of these were omitted, the resultant research findings could be unreliable. To avoid this error, all very large companies in such industries should be sampled (that is, a census taken of the stratum) plus a representative sample of smaller firms (this is discussed later).

Particular versions of probability sampling, for example *systematic (or quasi-) random, stratified random, cluster, area* and *multi-stage* may be feasible alternatives in some surveys. To check their suitability, the needs and conditions of individual surveys would have to be studied.

Quasi-random sampling
Quasi-random sampling is a widely used method: it uses a sampling frame and requires calculation of a sampling interval, obtained by finding the ratio of the population to the sample. For example, a population of 5,000 people and a sample of 125 might be involved: the sampling interval will be 5,000/125 = 40. A randomly selected number between 1 and 40 is chosen (say, 4), and the series then becomes 4, 44, 84 . . . until the sample size is complete. Those whose names occur in these specific positions would be interviewed.

Stratified random sampling
Stratified random sampling depends on suitable strata of the population under survey being identified. Within these defined strata, random selection takes place; significant characteristics (e.g. age, sex,

socio-economic groups) of the total population should be represented adequately in the different strata of the sample. Too many strata obviously complicate the survey, add little to the overall value of the findings and increase costs. Pilot surveys can help to identify characteristics relevant to a survey.

Cluster sampling
Cluster, or area, sampling, as the name suggests, occurs when interviews are concentrated in relatively small numbers of groups or clusters which are selected at random. Within these random clusters every unit is sampled. For example, in a national survey of company salesmen, sales territories would be identified and a random selection of these taken; every salesman would be interviewed.

Multi-stage sampling
Multi-stage sampling is useful where populations are widely dispersed: it involves selection at two or more successive stages. At each stage a sample (stratified or otherwise) is taken until the final sampling units are achieved. For example, the first stage of a national sample survey would be based on standard regions as classified by the Registrar General. Each region would be allocated interviews based on its population. The second stage would involve a selection of towns and rural districts; in the third stage a sample of individual respondents would be taken from the electoral registers of the second-stage area. This systematic process of sub-sampling could be refined further so that administrative areas would be divided into wards, then polling districts.

A four-stage sampling design is given in Table 3.1; it illustrates the sequential approach to building a representative sample of adults aged eighteen years and over in Britain.

Hence, the practical disadvantages of random or probability sampling may be minimized largely by using some of the alternative versions outlined earlier. Experienced market researchers are fully aware of the crucial importance of a sound sample design to the quality of the overall research effort and some ingenious sampling approaches have been devised. The British Market Research Bureau, for instance, has developed GRID, a method of sampling which combines some of the features of probability sampling with those of non-probability (quota) sampling.

The various stages in the development of an effective sample design are outlined in Figure 3.4. The first step (as discussed in the section dealing with the research brief) is to define clearly the population

Table 3.1 Four-stage representative sample of adults aged eighteen and over living in private households in Britain (south of the Caledonian Canal)

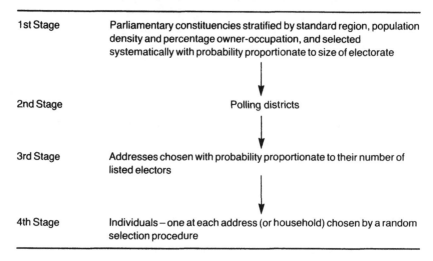

1st Stage	Parliamentary constituencies stratified by standard region, population density and percentage owner-occupation, and selected systematically with probability proportionate to size of electorate
2nd Stage	Polling districts
3rd Stage	Addresses chosen with probability proportionate to their number of listed electors
4th Stage	Individuals – one at each address (or household) chosen by a random selection procedure

under survey. Unless this is done accurately and agreed by all concerned with the survey, the value of the eventual survey report to a client may be reduced substantially. The nature of the problems and the needs of clients should be explained to researchers, so that they can develop relevant methodologies. In cases where sampling frames do not exist, it is necessary to exercise some ingenuity so that an effective sample can be drawn (see Table 3.2). As will be noted from Figure 3.4, a critical factor in the research process is deciding on an appropriate *sample size*.

The size of a sample affects the quality of the research data: it is *not* a question of applying some arbitrary percentage to a specific population. The process is (or should be) sophisticated; sample size depends on the basic characteristics of the population, the type of information required and, of course, the costs entailed. The larger the sample size, the greater its precision or reliability, but practical constraints of time, staff and cost intervene. Budgetary restrictions are particularly influential in deciding how large a sample can be taken. Cost and accuracy are closely linked, so sponsors should be told of the interaction of these factors if they are demanding to have almost instant information from a hastily devised survey.

When computing the size of a sample the non-response factor should be borne in mind. If, for instance, a final sample of 2,500 is

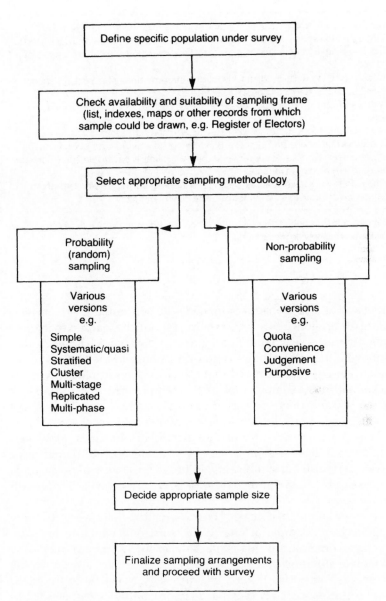

Figure 3.4 Sequential approach to developing sample design

Table 3.2 Sampling procedures for survey of health and disability in UK town

---

1. No reliable and complete sampling frame of the disabled in this town existed
2. Although strict random sampling would not be feasible, every effort would be made to secure a sample which would be representative of disabled persons in the age group 16–74
3. In each of the 117 polling districts, the first five street names alphabetically (ignoring hospitals and similar institutions) were selected
4. Within each street the third person (a number one to five drawn at random) was selected
5. The house numbers for interviewing were those of the third people listed
6. The above drill resulted in 117 × 5 = 585 residences listed in order; every thirteenth and fourteenth were kept as reserves starting with number seven (a number between one and ten selected at random)
7. Where there were fewer than two persons on the electoral roll in a street, the third person in that street and the next street were taken together

---

Note: This systematic method of initial contact was complemented by standardized instructions on interviewing procedures.

planned and non-response is estimated at 20 per cent, it would be wise to inflate the original figure to 3,000. But it should be realized that while this maintains the size of the final sample and so helps its precision, it cannot avoid the bias arising from non-response in the first instance.

Statistically, it can be proved that the error of a sample is inversely proportional to the square root of the sample size. For example, a sample of 4,000 is only *twice* as accurate as a sample of 1,000 (sample size is increased fourfold; the square root of 4 is 2). Hence, to double the accuracy of a sample, it must be increased four times. However, after a certain size of sample has been achieved, additional large increases in size do not significantly improve the statistical precision of a given sample. Field survey costs, of course, increase directly with larger samples.

If a population had basic characteristics that were entirely homogeneous, a sample of one would suffice in which to measure these characteristics; but this is hardly ever likely. Where, however, considerable differences, that is, hetereogeneity, occur, a large sample is necessary. Computing the size of a sample is, as will be appreciated, a complex process; each survey needs to be carefully evaluated for its individual requirements.

With random sampling it is possible to calculate mathematically the size of a sample in order to achieve data of a stated degree of precision.

This involves the evaluation of a confidence coefficient which indicates the specified degree of certainty with which a particular sample estimate can be accepted as a true estimator of the population parameters or values. A level of confidence of 95 per cent (which implies a probability of 0·95) would result in a 5 per cent level of significance, while a 99 per cent confidence level (0·99 probability) would result in a 1 per cent level of significance. These two levels are the most commonly used in practical research and full details of the statistical theory underlying confidence intervals and the mathematical function of normal distribution will be found in specialized texts (see selective reading list in Appendix C). Since sample values are only estimators of true, but unknown, population values, the average or mean values obtained from sampling procedures inevitably involve some measure of sampling error.

It is not possible to know precisely the sampling error in a particular instance unless the population value is known – which, of course, is decidedly unlikely. However, the degree to which numerical data (i.e. sets of sample values) tend to be distributed about an average or mean value is known as the dispersion or variation; a widely used measure of this variation is termed the standard deviation, which plays an important role in evaluating the reliability of sampling data. The standard deviation of a sampling distribution, i.e. the frequency distribution of all the estimates taken as the result of sampling a certain population, is termed the standard error of the mean (SE). If this statistic is large, then the sample estimate of the population will vary considerably; if it is small, it can reasonably be assumed to be a good and reliable estimate. (Further exploration of these aspects of research design occur in the recommended texts.) In developing an effective sample design, common sense as well as statistical competence is clearly called for. With simple random samples, the formula for calculating sample size (n) is as follows.

Basic statistical notation

	Population	Sample
Average or mean	μ	$\bar{x}$
Standard deviation	σ	s
Variance	σ^2	s^2

Note: Greek letters = population parameters
    Italic letters = sample statistics

Taking $\qquad SE_{\bar{x}} = \dfrac{\sigma}{\sqrt{n}}$

Inverting it $\qquad \sqrt{n} = \dfrac{\sigma}{SE_{\bar{x}}}$ $\qquad\qquad$ (3.1)

Therefore, $\qquad n = \dfrac{\sigma^2}{SE^2_{\bar{x}}}$

The above formula assumes that the standard deviation in the population is available or, failing that, it is possible to take the standard deviation in the sample as a reasonable estimate of it. In addition, it is necessary to know the size of the standard error which can be tolerated.

An alternative formula for calculating the sample size of a simple random sample is as follows.

$$n = \left(\frac{Z\hat{\sigma}}{E} \right)^2 \qquad\qquad (3.2)$$

Where: n = sample size;
$\qquad Z$ = Z-statistic corresponding to the desired confidence level (1.96 in example below);
$\qquad \sigma$ = the estimated value of the standard deviation of the population parameter, usually estimated from a pilot study/survey (12 in example below);
$\qquad E$ = the maximum acceptable magnitude of error (2.0 in example below).

Example
What size of sample, by random process, would be required to give a 0.95 probability that a sample mean of a sales team's productivity would be within 2.0 points of the true mean? Assume $S = 12$.

Since $0.95 = 95\%$ confidence level $= 1.96Z$ value,

therefore, $1.96 \times \dfrac{S}{\sqrt{n}} = 2.0$ $\qquad\qquad$ (3.3)

$\qquad 1.96 \times \dfrac{12}{\sqrt{n}} = 2.0$

$\qquad \dfrac{1.96 \times 12}{2.0} = \sqrt{n}$

$\therefore n = 138$ salesmen would need to be surveyed.

SUMMARY

Five logical steps are identifiable in the marketing research process: research brief; research proposal; data collection; data analysis and evaluation; and preparation and presentation of research report. All stages demand efficiency and sensitivity to bias.

Sampling methodology is the foundation of the research design: a sample is a microcosm of the population from which it is drawn. Two main types of sample exist: random (probability) and quota (non-probability): the former is widely used by research bodies because of its superior theoretical basis. However, it requires a sampling frame and few exist. Several versions of probability samples occur and reduce problems in practice. Quota sampling is simpler, faster and more prone to bias; it is widely used in evaluating research where its handicaps are well controlled.

Computing an effective sample size is complex; it is not merely a percentage of some population. It depends on the basic characteristics of the population, type of information sought and costs: each survey needs careful evaluation.

4

Research tools

Primary and secondary data

As seen earlier, data for market investigation can be collected at two levels: primary and secondary.

After carefully assessing the secondary data gathered by means of desk research through consulting official publications, trade surveys and so on, it may be found that sufficient knowledge has been acquired to enable specific marketing decisions to be taken within acceptable levels of risk. If more information is desirable, then primary data collection has to be organized.

Primary data collection

As observed in Chapter 3, primary data collection involves the gathering of information for the first time by either one, or a blend of, observation, experimentation and questionnaires. A multi-technique approach to primary research involves the use of a combination of some of these research tools in order to reduce the incidence of bias associated with a single technique. Unfortunately, bias can creep into research in many ways and everything should be done to keep it closely in check.

Observation
Observation has been described as the classical method of investigation; widely practised by, for example, doctors, scientists and social

investigators, it is also of value in marketing surveys, provided that it is well devised and controlled. For example, noting how people actually go about shopping and the selection of specific products and brands; studying how tools are used in the work place; traffic counts. 'Unobtrusive measures' of observation have included hidden video cameras, one-way mirrors, TV audit services, panel research (home audit), assessment of wear and tear of flooring in display areas. Poster advertising sites are checked for their maintenance and correctness. Considerable ingenuity has often been displayed in collecting qualitative information as well as gathering quantitative estimates. One of the pioneers of market and social research in the UK – Mass Observation – founded by Tom Harrison in the 1930s, popularized the technique of observational methodology.

Experimentation
Experimentation – closely related to observational techniques – may apply some of the principles of scientific investigation in an attempt to understand better the likely responses to several alternatives in the marketing mix. Variations of product (flavour, colour); packaging (different styles and/or sizes); advertising (restricted; extensive; various media mixes); distribution strategies (direct, agents); price (differential pricing, e.g. based on quantities) – may all be subject to some degree of experimentation, perhaps in carefully selected test markets or in simulated shopping conditions, such as 'hall tests'. Computer modelling may be particularly useful in acquiring a better understanding of the interactions between variables, for example when certain changes are made to prices in specific product markets.

Questionnaire methodologies

Questionnaires are extensively used in surveys of all kinds. They can be administered by telephone, mail or through personal interviewing.

Questionnaires by personal interviewing
This methodology is attractive because of its versatility, relative speed and economy. Constructing a questionnaire is a task which demands considerable expertise; a popular approach to questionnaire construction involves 'funnelling'. (See Figure 4.1.) This technique is advisable because it reduces the likelihood of bias which may arise from more direct approaches. The type of questionnaire will depend on the nature

'Funnel' technique*

From most general questions gradually
focusing down to some specific
and restricted questions

'Inverted funnel' technique

From specific questions first and thence
opening up to more general questions.
Compared with 'funnelling', little-used

*e.g. general opinions about subject;

specific knowledge of subject area;

direct questions about particular kinds of product/service

Direct questions about specific brand of product

e.g. Have you heard or seen any advertisements for cars recently?
              If YES
    Were any of these advertisements for imported cars?
              If YES
    Were any of these advertisements on television?
              If YES
    Were any of these advertisements for X brand of car?
              If YES
    What did the advertisements say?

Figure 4.1   Planned sequence of questions

of the problem investigated, the kind of population sampled and the sample size.

Although questionnaires are an attractive method of gathering information, they have drawbacks: people may refuse to reply or give invalid answers either accidentally or intentionally; researchers may distort questions or record answers incorrectly. Respondents must be able to understand the questions (hence questions should be phrased in language readily comprehensible to specific kinds of respondents); they should be capable of answering the questions put to them (i.e. they should have knowledge of the subject under survey); and respondents should be willing to participate in the survey. It is vital for those organizing surveys to take care that questions are within the competence of specific respondents; they need to take account of their 'frames of reference', so that, for example, words are used within the intellectual, cultural and social experiences of individuals.

Questionnaires need to be devised with the objectives of the research firmly in mind; every question should have a purpose and should add to the general quality of the investigation.

Again, it is necessary to refer to the problems of bias; this, unfortunately, also intrudes into question construction (and also the questioning process). For example, respondents should not feel social pressure to answer a question in some particular way which might involve assessment of health or social habits, patterns of advertising viewing. Some years ago a survey investigated readership of *Gone with the Wind*; to the question 'Have you read this book?', an excessively high number responded 'Yes'. When the question was rephrased to 'Do you intend to read *Gone with the Wind*?', a far lower, and more valid, level of response was achieved. Those who had not read it were reluctant to say so, but they felt more comfortable with giving a truer picture of their behaviour when the question no longer carried a certain degree of social stigma.

Every question in a questionnaire should be vetted for possible bias, e.g. suggesting expectations of behaviour which would put respondents 'on their guard'.

Information for marketing decision making is frequently sought over several areas of buying activity (see Figures 2.4 and 3.2).

Major areas of measurement

1. Consumption patterns; market trends (reasons for market changes).
2. Beliefs about specific products/services.
3. Expectations related to specific products/services (define benefits sought).
4. Attitudes – general and specific.
5. Motivations – buying behaviour (influence of family buying habits; industrial group decision making, etc.); nature of motivations (economic, psychological, social, etc.).
6. Competitors' activities (define and classify principal competition; assess their strategies and tactics, etc.).
7. Media exposure and influence.
8. Classification of buyers (present and prospective).

In Chapter 3 some specific guides have been given in order to focus research productively.

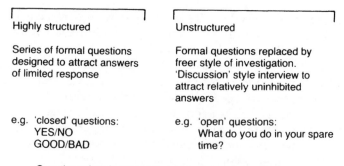

Highly structured	Unstructured
Series of formal questions designed to attract answers of limited response	Formal questions replaced by freer style of investigation. 'Discussion' style interview to attract relatively uninhibited answers
e.g. 'closed' questions: YES/NO GOOD/BAD	e.g. 'open' questions: What do you do in your spare time?

Questionnaires frequently 'mix' the styles of questioning

Figure 4.2   Questionnaire continuum

Structured and unstructured questionnaires
Questionnaires may be highly structured – with a series of formal questions designed to attract answers of limited response – or unstructured, where formal questions are replaced by a freer style of investigation; the interviewer encourages conversation to develop, guiding it by means of an 'interviewing guide' or check-list of the main topics of the enquiry. (See Figure 4.2 and section on Interviewing in this chapter.) In practice, questionnaires are frequently hybrid; the essential purpose of surveys is to attract valid and reliable data, so flexibility in approach is desirable. Different survey populations call for variations in questioning techniques (see Appendix B for examples of questionnaires).

It is important that respondents should give valid answers; in some cases they may not know enough about the issue or product being investigated to give a reliable response. In such cases, interviewers may have to be content to enter 'Don't Know', which indicates the importance of including this category in potential answers listed in a questionnaire. Prompting of respondents' recall of particular buying behaviour of brands may be admissible, but it should be used with great care to avoid bias. Respondents often want to be 'helpful' and give answers which they think will satisfy interviewers. Of course, there are a few who will deliberately distort their responses to specific questions but these are usually detected by 'check' questions planted in a questionnaire.

Qualitative studies have shown that direct questioning is often a fairly blunt tool and less direct methods, for example group discussion, are more likely to reveal the true motivation and behaviour of respondents. (See page 43, Qualitative research.)

Pilot testing

Pilot testing of questionnaires is critical for successful surveying. From this process will come clues for rewriting questions, changing their sequence or style of composition. As stated earlier, questions should be phrased in language which is readily understood by specific kinds of respondents whose vocabularies may be distinctly limited. Even one word can radically change the whole impact of a question, as an American health study found when matched sets of respondents were given alternative forms of a question, changed by one word only, as follows:

1. 'Do you think anything should be done to make it easier for people to pay hospital or doctor bills?' (82 per cent 'YES'.)

2. 'Should' replaced by 'could'. (77 per cent 'YES'.)

3. 'Should' replaced by 'might'. (63 per cent 'YES'.)

In the case of personal interviewing, stress on specific words may result in biased responses.

Finally, questionnaires are probably the most widely known and used market research tool. Their popularity and flexibility have not always resulted in high standards of research. That 'you get the data you deserve' should be a warning against carelessly drafted questionnaires, which may mislead management instead of providing valid, reliable guides for decision making.

Telephone surveys

A rapidly growing tool of market investigation involves surveys by telephone of both consumers and industrial markets. The comparative ease with which telephone calls can be made as opposed to the physical difficulties of locating and interviewing respondents face to face may sometimes delude prospective users. First, an effective sample must be developed and a questionnaire designed to present respondents with a series of well-structured, readily understood questions which follow a logical sequence. Secondly, the telephone interviewer requires special training to ensure that questions are presented clearly and that responses are accurately recorded.

Telephone surveys are clearly limited to those populations which have universal access to telephones. Although rented domestic telephones have increased significantly in the UK there is still some way to go before all homes are equipped. Other problems arise because of ex-directory subscribers (probably 5 per cent in the UK, but considerably more in US urban areas) and 'removals' since the last issue of telephone directories and so on.

The advantages of the telephone as a research tool are, briefly, that it is convenient; imperative; confers anonymity; attracts freer response; can be used at precise times; can be readily controlled and supervised; speed of data collection. Disadvantages of this technique also exist; they are: limits to communication – no visual clues to assist questioning; potential wastage because of unobtainable numbers or crossed lines.

A particularly productive use of telephone surveying occurs with *central telephone interviewing* facilities which are now operated by nearly 100 research companies in the UK. A special Telephone Research Interest Group has been founded in association with the Market Research Society, the leading professional body dedicated to the maintenance of professional standards in the practice of market research of all kinds.

Computer-assisted telephone interviewing (CATI)

CATI is a developing method of gathering survey data through linking computer technology and telecommunications, thus eliminating paper questionnaires. Various types of CATI have been developed but they all have a common basic procedure: an interviewer reads the question (which is displayed on a VDU) to the telephoned respondent, and the answer is recorded by keyboard; several UK research firms now operate versions of CATI. Although CATI can steer respondents through fairly complex sequences of questioning, it seems to be distinctly limited in its ability to handle open-ended questions.

Another technological development covers *direct computer interviewing* (DCI), where the respondent interacts directly with the computer instead of through the medium of an interviewer. Both CATI and DCI share the same technology, but the former is controlled by professional interviewers while the latter depends solely on respondents to make the inputs themselves.

Telephone surveys may be particularly useful in the early stages of surveys when, for example, it may be necessary to eliminate non-users of a particular product or service. This may be advantageous to industrial market researchers, when enquiries are concerned with users' experience of specific kinds of equipment. They can also be effective where enquiries are relatively limited both in scope and in the time taken to respond. It is important to speak to the person who can give valid information; it is not always easy to locate industrial respondents and, even when this has been done, to encourage them to dedicate time to an immediate survey. Diplomatic skills should be exercised to attract co-operation; a call-back at a more convenient time may well secure data which could otherwise not be readily available.

Mail surveys

Mail surveys are limited in their effectiveness: although superficially attractive in terms of costs, their true value should be related to *effective* response rates, which are generally very low. Non-response is not a random process, so considerable hidden biases may be present in the eventual survey findings.

The general principles of sound questionnaire construction are particularly important with mail surveys because they are by their nature impersonal and lack the advantages of face-to-face interviewing. Questionnaires have to be self-contained; this means that respondents should find no difficulty in understanding the questions and in following the printed instructions guiding them through sequences of alternative responses. Simple guides, such as 'If NO, please go to question 5', should be inserted. Definitions of property, for example, should be clear to all respondents, so that answers are similarly based: 'In counting bedrooms, exclude toilet and bathroom'.

Time intervals should be explicitly stated; for instance, a 'week' or 'month' should be qualified to ensure consistency of responses. In the case of trading companies, it is important to qualify terms such as 'sales' – does this refer to orders booked, invoiced sales or sales invoiced and paid for? References to sales turnover should be explained: does it refer, for example, to calendar years or trading years? – unless this is clearly understood, respondents may well use different periods of time and render comparative data unreliable.

Every detail of a mail questionnaire requires attention: layout and printing are particularly important. Good quality paper (printed on one side only) should be used. The overall design of the enquiry should result in an attractive format, with questions well-spaced and easy to read. Wherever possible questionnaires should be mailed to an identified individual (with their name and title correctly spelled). A covering letter should outline the nature and purpose of the survey and invite respondents to cooperate. Confidentiality should be assured; it is advisable to indicate why the respondent has been approached, so a simple statement of the method of sampling might reassure those who wonder why they have been approached. In the

37

use of industrial or trade enquiries, the offer of a summary of some of the principal findings of the survey has been known to encourage cooperation. Reply-paid facilities should, of course, be included with the survey form.

The impersonal nature of mail surveys means that answers have to be accepted as written unless, of course, some particularly interesting responses merit follow-up telephone interviews. In some instances it has been found productive to telephone beforehand, to introduce the survey and obtain assurances of willing involvement in it.

Response rates should be monitored by researchers and arrangements made for follow-ups to increase these to acceptable levels. Follow-up reminders should be tactfully worded – after all, informants are often busy people, doubtless receive several questionnaires, some of which are of little direct interest to them, and their involvement in the survey is voluntary.

It is common practice to send two reminders to non-respondents, usually at about 14-day intervals. Inevitably, responses decline over time and a decision has to be taken to 'close the books' and assess the overall result. If a very low response rate characterizes a particular survey, then serious thought should be given to its validity. If, for example, a 12½ per cent response rate was achieved, it follows that of nearly 90 per cent of the specific sample population nothing is known except that they failed to respond. It might be possible to telephone a random subsample of non-respondents and obtain some data which would augment the survey. Perhaps they would be willing to complete a simplified version of the original enquiry? At this late stage of the survey response rates are not likely to improve very much; this stresses the need, as mentioned earlier, of detailed planning coupled with a creative approach.

Various experiments have been conducted to increase response rates to mail surveys: they have included small monetary inducements (to be handled delicately: too large a sum might be considered a bribe; too small a sum an insult); gifts such as ballpoint pens, diaries, etc; appeals to altruism or professionalism, as with surveys of significant interest to members of professional organizations such as the Law Society or the BMA. Anonymity seems to be a particularly effective means of securing high responses from professionals such as accountants, especially where enquiries may cover sensitive issues.

To sum up: mail questionnaires are useful where the sample population is widely dispersed or difficult to contact because of professional commitments. However, response rates are generally low; reminders extend the time for completion of the survey, so speed

Table 4.1 Comparative attributes of alternative data collection methods

	Telephone questionnaire	Mail questionnaire	Personal interviewing
Collecting complex information	L	?	H
Obtaining qualitative insight, e.g. through observation of respondents and environment	L	L	H
Attracting respondent–Interviewer bias	?	L	H
Gathering extra information, e.g. by probing	L	?	H
Controlling interview situation	?	L	H
Effecting satisfactory response rate	H	L	H
Reaching widely scattered sample	H	H	L
Completing survey relatively speedily	H	L	?
Economic cost	H	L	?

H = Comparatively high
L = Comparatively low
? = Possible
Note: Obviously some methods may score differently in certain circumstances, and in some instances more than one survey technique could be used.

is not necessarily a marked feature. In addition, costs must be assessed realistically, that is against the *actual* responses received; these may be at a level that results in a much more expensive survey than was originally envisaged. Questionnaires, as always, should be carefully pilot-tested to ensure that they are fully understood and capable of being answered with a reasonable degree of effort.

Table 4.1 presents a comparative analysis of the three principal methods of gathering data from questionnaires. Some methods may score differently in certain circumstances and in some instances more than one survey technique could be used (see earlier discussion on multi-technique research strategy, this chapter).

Interviewing

Personal or face-to-face interviewing is a core function of marketing research; much of the quality of the entire research process rests on its effectiveness. Despite the growth in popularity of telephone and mail surveys, personal interviewing retains its long-held dominance across a wide spectrum of surveys – market, social, political.

Variety of interviewing techniques

Techniques can range from formal, structured interviews to informal discussions with individuals or selected groups of informants. With the former type, standardized questions in a carefully planned sequence are administered by interviewers who do not vary from their trained routine. In the latter case there may be no formal questioning: the group leader or facilitator will encourage discussion relevant to an agreed topic of defined interest to develop. Between these broad divisions of interviewing, variations exist: the nature of a survey focus and the data needed to explore its problems will influence the methodology used.

Interviewing is a social process; it involves an interaction between the interviewer and the respondent. It is important that this interaction – which is established very quickly – should result in a successful interview, that is, in the collection of relevant, reliable data. The psychological atmosphere of an interview is, therefore, immensely influential in the process of communication between interviewer and respondent. Flexibility is an important factor in successful inter-viewing.

Three forms of interviewing can be identified as follows.

1. Limited response: the questions are generally limited in scope and in the information required: closed questions predominate.
2. Free response: the interview is much more 'open'; discussion is encouraged by the facilitator who carefully reduces irrelevancies to a minimum.
3. Defensive response: interviewers may exert pressure on inform-ants who are expected to defend their beliefs, attitudes, etc. This belligerent style may be counter-productive and has been widely

criticized as contrary to the establishment of a productive interaction between the interview parties.

Interviewers' general responsibilities

1. To locate informants who fulfil the needs of the chosen method of sampling.
2. To translate these contacts into effective interviews.
3. To secure valid and reliable responses.
4. To record responses accurately.

The above are demanding tasks: interviewers experience fatigue, both psychological and physical, so particular attention should be given to their selection, training, motivation and supervision in order to maintain consistently high standards of interviewing.

Leading survey organizations such as the Government Social Survey, AGB and the British Market Research Bureau pay particular heed to the quality of their interviewing force. In 1968, the Market Research Society published a special guide to the selection of effective interviewers.

The supervision of field interviewers is vital and, again, is a matter of concern. Experienced and reputable research organizations such as the BBC Audience Research Department operate well-organized systems of interviewer supervision on a regional basis. Unfortunately, the quality of interviewing in some market surveys falls short of the high standards set by leading organizations. It is clearly futile to devise elaborate research designs if the interviewers who will have the responsibility for eliciting and recording respondents' reactions are not adequately selected, trained and motivated. It is advisable, therefore, to (i) check the types of interviewers to be used in a specific survey (they should be matched to the needs of the survey); and (ii) check how these interviewers are recruited, trained, motivated and supervised (morale is affected by professional commitment and pay).

Computer-assisted personal interviewing (CAPI)
This development of CATI (see earlier section on telephone interviewing) has been pioneered in the UK by Research International. It involves laptop computers, by means of which researchers conducting personal interviews can input data and feed the results via the telephone, thus reducing dramatically the whole research process.

Bias – a perennial problem of designing and conducting surveys –

also affects the process of interviewing. This problem was acknow-ledged in the MRS report quoted earlier, when it was felt that the attitude of interviewers to the concept of market research was a very important factor in influencing the objectivity and quality of the interview. Biases can arise in many ways, some of which may, unfortunately, not be identified, so every care should be taken to eliminate possible sources.

The 'interviewer effect' occurs when influence of an interviewer on a respondent is such that it results in inaccurate, biased responses to specific questions. Respondents may feel ill at ease with interviewers who are evidently not of their social class or ethnic origin; research findings are not, however, entirely definitive.

As observed in the section on questionnaires (this chapter), respon-dents may be unwilling to give correct answers, perhaps from ignorance or difficulty in self-expression. Interviewers need to be sensitive to such issues and encourage valid responses while shrewdly assessing the value of some responses. The 'accommodating answer' may sometimes be given, perhaps because the question was poorly phrased and had some of the elements of a 'leading' question, that is, one which tends to suggest the type of preferred response. Knowing the identity of a survey sponsor may bias responses, so interviewers should ensure that a client's name is not revealed.

In the case of quota sampling (see sampling section), interviewers have the responsibility of choosing informants who may be classified by stratification factors such as age, sex, socio-economic group and geographical location. The widespread and long-established use of socio-economic groupings A–E (see Chapter 6) has serious disadvant-ages as well as distinct advantages. Among its disadvantages is the opportunity for bias to intrude because interviewers may select respondents to fill certain socio-economic quotas who do not have identical attributes. Experienced interviewers are less likely to be misled, but the potential danger of bias exists. As a practical step in reducing this bias, the Market Research Society published in 1990 *Occupation Groupings: a Job Dictionary*, which lists thousands of jobs in alphabetical order with their relevant socio-economic grades. This guide is available in a compact size suitable for interviewers to carry with them.

Finally, another serious source of bias is non-response and, as discussed in the sampling section, every effort must be made to control this factor through improved sample design and interviewing tech-niques.

Interviewer identity card

In 1987 the Market Research Society introduced the MRS Interviewer Identity Card system in order to safeguard respondents to market surveys. A member of the public can be reassured when an interviewer displays this card when requesting an interview. This well-devised scheme has the enthusiastic support of the leading research organizations: it forms part of the MRS code of conduct (discussed later).

Qualitative research

In Chapter 2, the complexity of modern patterns of consumption was illustrated by an outline model (Figure 2.4), and the need to collect both quantitative and qualitative information about buying behaviour was stressed.

Essence of qualitative research

Qualitative research aims to give insights into perception, motivation and attitudes – to answer: what? why? how? Its findings are often described, rather pejoratively, as 'soft' data and contrasted with 'hard' data originating from quantitative studies, but both kinds of data are valuable in order to acquire a fuller understanding of markets and the people who buy and sell in them. Hard data are not necessarily superior to non-numeric data; ideally, they are complementary.

The essence of qualitative research is that it is diagnostic; it explores certain kinds of behaviour, for example, brand loyalty, and seeks explanations. It probes rather than counts; intrinsically, it is subjective for its findings cannot be supported by rigorous statistical tests. But, as the Market Research Society noted in 1979, qualitative research provides the constant conceptual link between consumers and decision makers in marketing and advertising development.

The structured, standardized techniques of quantitative research result in highly useful sets of statistics on consumption but they fail to provide answers of more subtlety and sophistication. Qualitative research is unstructured, flexible, and oblique; it is a term rather freely used to describe several specific kinds of marketing research, such as exploratory research, depth interviewing, opinion research and so on.

Typical techniques

Typical techniques are group discussions, focus groups and depth interviews which are based on small non-random samples.

Depth interviews

Depth interviews are one of the principal methods of qualitative research. Basically, they are non-directive, informal interviews – more conversational in nature than traditional interviews – in which respondents are encouraged to talk about the subject rather than provide 'yes' or 'no' answers to specific questions. The relaxed atmosphere surrounding such interviews can be used creatively by an experienced investigator to explore motivations and attitudes, for instance, sometimes related to topics of some sensitivity. A 'funnelling' approach may be adopted (see questionnaire section, this chapter).

This type of interview sometimes takes place with *groups of individuals*, as people tend to be less inhibited in a group. Sessions are usually tape-recorded for later analysis. Expert direction of the group is vital; the discussion leader should have psychological training and be sensitive to the dynamics of a group and to the value of remarks, which though not appearing to be directly relevant to the subject under discussion may reveal significant clues to subconscious motivations.

Group discussions may involve between seven and nine people and last up to 1½ hours. Individual interviews may take between 30 and 60 minutes.

Focus groups/extended creativity groups (ECGs)

Focus groups and ECGs are derivations of group depth interviewing, and have been used to explore user behaviour in horticultural and agricultural markets. ECGs have been combined with depth discussions in various consumer market investigations, including the study of the prescription habits of medical general practitioners. Group discussions have been proved valuable in understanding people's attitudes towards the consumption of specific kinds of food, alcoholic drinks, etc. They have been instrumental in providing clues for advertising copy, packaging design, product formulations, etc.

Qualitative research may be particularly valuable and effective in developing countries, which lack reliable sources of data and whose patterns of consumption may be profoundly influenced by cultural factors.

Projective techniques

In the 1950s a battery of behavioural science research techniques was imported into market research, sometimes under the impressive if misleading title of motivation research. Some flamboyant claims were made by its disciples, whose methodologies and conclusions eventually lost popularity, particularly because they tended to lack practicality. Of the various techniques used to some extent in market research are the following.

Word association test
An informant is given a single word (say, 'breakfast') and asked to say immediately what other words come to mind. A series of words in quick succession would be fired at the respondent. Household products, for instance, prepared meals or cleaning compounds might be researched and clues gathered which could help advertising campaigns, etc.

Sentence completion test
Similar to word association, this also relies on the spontaneity of responses. Informants are invited to complete, under pressure, a number of sentences; for example, 'People who drink instant coffee are . . .'.

Thematic apperception test (TAT)
This presents informants with a series of cartoons depicting, perhaps, a woman buying cosmetics, and they are asked to describe that person. Interpretation should be done by skilled researchers.

Cartoons (blank balloons)
Associated with sentence completion tests and TATs, this test involves a cartoon or sketch of two people in a particular setting, such as shop assistant and customer. One of the character's words are in a 'special balloon'; the other's balloon is empty and informants are invited to give the reply which is considered suitable for the occasion. Other qualitative research techniques which could help to generate concepts for new products include the following.

Special techniques
Gap analysis
A simple perceptual model of a specific market is constructed and consumers invited to respond to a series of attitudinal measurements related, for example, to a particular brand.

Action studies
A panel of housewives might be asked to keep a 'diary' of their cooking habits (listing products, brands, methods of usage).

45

Brainstorming
A method of idea generation from the late 1930s – based on the spontaneous contribution of ideas by a group focusing on a specific subject or problem. During this early stage no judgement or evaluation is made; later, analysis may reveal suggestions for new product concepts.

Synectics
The aim is to encourage people to view problems in a new light; to break free from hide-bound perceptions and reactions and to look anew at familiar objects or methods of operation.

Attractions and potential hazards of qualitative research

Qualitative research has many attractions; it is relatively low-cost compared with quantitative enquiries; also, it is generally much quicker and flexible. Its applications are widening: industry, local government services and health care are all new areas in which qualitative research has been productive. On the other hand, its critics point with concern to the small sample sizes and methods of selecting participants which may adversely affect the validity of its methodologies and findings.

Attitude research

The distinctions between attitude research and qualitative research tend to be blurred and some overlap is virtually inevitable. In practice, researchers generally measure attitudes by means of attitude scales and related techniques such as semantic differential scales. Projective techniques, as just discussed, may also be used for studying motivation.

Two crucial factors concern all research activities and specifically the measurement of attitudes: *validity* – the extent to which the scale is free from both random and systematic error and measures what it is supposed to measure; and *reliability* – which relates to the consistency of the measuring technique, i.e. that repeated measurements under the same conditions will give the same results. A certain scale may possess reliability but it may not be valid for a specific research project; the former attribute is easier to check than the latter. Techniques such as construct validity, content validity and predictive validity are used to evaluate the validity of a particular selling method.

Relevance of attitudes
Attitudes have particular significance for marketing researchers and strategists; they do not guarantee that certain types of behaviour will happen, but they are useful guides as to likely behaviour in certain circumstances.

Attitudes are characterized by a predisposition or state of readiness to act or react, in a favourable or unfavourable way, to certain stimuli. They form relatively enduring systems; they are not innate but develop with learning. Opinions and attitudes are closely related: the former have been described as verbalized attitudes. Attitudes influence everyone and affect the ways individuals perceive other people, objects (including products) and events. They are regarded as having three components: cognitive (beliefs, knowledge specific to the object of an attitude); affective (feelings – positive or negative); and conative (action tendency – readiness to display particular behaviour).

The characteristics of attitudes, including their formation and susceptibility to change, and the nature of the relationship between attitudes and behaviour, are complex considerations and have been studied in depth by psychologists over many years. As far as marketers are concerned, some ready appreciation of the principal and well-tried methods of attitude measurement should prove helpful.

Leading scaling techniques
Attitude scales are of several types; provided that the scales are well devised, the resultant information can give more sensitive insight into, for example, consumption preferences, than can be gathered from using dichotomous questions such as YES/NO or BUY/DON'T BUY. Four generic types of scales exist.

Nominal scales
These are the simplest of the four generic types: they involve nothing more than simple classification by certain attributes which are then quantified, as in the case of populations analysed by age and sex. No gradation or distance between such groups is implied. In a market survey questions might be concerned with ownership of some consumer durable and data listed from YES/NO responses.

Ordinal scales
Also known as ranking scales, these are commonly used in psychology and sociology. In marketing research products could be ranked according to certain criteria, such as taste, freshness or convenient packaging. 'Paired comparisons' may be made between two sets of objects at a time and statistical tests applied to the ranked data. It is important to realize that ranking merely provides measures of position or order; it does not imply that the 'steps' between ranks are equal. Ranking or ordinal scales are, therefore, limited to measures such as median, quartile or percentile.

Interval scales
Unlike ordinal scales, these use equal units of measurement which make it possible to give not only positional values but also the distances between individual scores. The most commonly used interval scales are those recording temperature. However, while the difference between scale positions is identical, for instance between 3 and 4, and 8 and 9, it is not correct to say that score 9 has three times the strength of score 3. To take a marketing example, if three competitive products are being evaluated for buying preferences and the first scores the highest at, say, 6, the second scores 3 and the third scores 2, it cannot be said that the first product is twice as much liked as the second one, because in an interval scale the zero point is fixed arbitrarily. In this particular case, it can be stated that the first product is more favoured than the others and that the degree of preference between the first and the second product is three times more than that existing between the second and third products.

Ratio scales
These have fixed origin or zero points, which allow all arithmetical operations to be used. Many marketing measurements possess the properties of a ratio scale, for example sales, market share, number of customers and so on, because in each instance a natural or absolute zero exists.

Rating scales
Those which measure by means of ordinal, interval or ratio scales; they can be verbal, diagrammatic or numerical. Some specific attitude scaling techniques are:

(1) *Likert scales* – a type of verbal rating scale in which respondents are asked how much they agree or disagree with a series of specific statements, for example:

'Advertising increases the price we have to pay for products';
'Advertising is an important source of information for consumers'.
Statements are scored thus:

Statements	Strongly agree	Agree	Uncertain	Disagree	Strongly disagree
'Positive' +	5	4	3	2	1
'Negative' −	1	2	3	4	5

High scores represent favourable attitudes to advertising: lower total
scores indicate unfavourable attitudes. But a given total score may
have different meanings, because of the different distribution of
individual scores. Some researchers favour modified scoring:

Agree strongly	*Agree slightly*	*Neither agree nor disagree*	*Disagree slightly*	*Disagree strongly*

(2) *Semantic differential scales* (Osgood Scales) – these popular diagrammatic rating scales are flexible, reasonably reliable, simple to use
and usually consist of 5- or 7-point scales with each extreme defined by
adjective or adjectival phrase. It is important that bipolar terms define
accurately the difference between two extreme feelings. Respondents
are asked to rate each of a number of objects or concepts along a
continuum, but it should not be assumed that the 5 (or 7) points on the
continuum are equally spaced. Typical values are:

 active/passive
 masculine/feminine
 savoury/tasteless
 hard/soft
 new/old
 good/bad
 weak/strong
 important/unimportant
 false/true

usual/unusual
slow/fast
beautiful/ugly

Descriptive phrases are:

up-to-date styling/out-of-date styling
really modern/ old fashioned
reasonably priced/ not reasonably priced
extravagant to use/economic to use
careful shopper/free-and-easy shopper
expense account car/family man's car
sturdy looking/doesn't look well built

Semantic scales can be monopolar (reasonably priced/not reasonably priced) or bipolar (slow/fast). The positions of positive and of bipolar scale should be randomized to minimize bias due to regular positioning. Comparative evaluations can be shown diagrammatically (see Figure 4.3). Semantic scales have been used in many enquiries, e.g. models of cars, retail stores, holiday tours, financial services, etc.

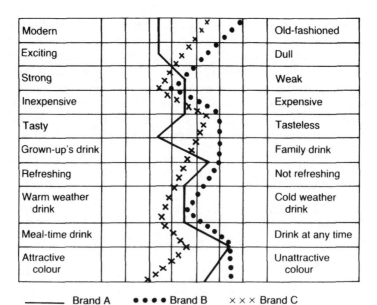

Modern	Old-fashioned
Exciting	Dull
Strong	Weak
Inexpensive	Expensive
Tasty	Tasteless
Grown-up's drink	Family drink
Refreshing	Not refreshing
Warm weather drink	Cold weather drink
Meal-time drink	Drink at any time
Attractive colour	Unattractive colour

———— Brand A   ● ● ● ● Brand B   × × × Brand C

Figure 4.3 Brand profile: beverage

SUMMARY

Primary data collection uses one or, ideally, a blend of observation, experimentation and questionnaires.

Questionnaires are widely used: they can be highly structured (closed questions) or unstructured (open questions/discussions).

Pilot testing is imperative.

Telephone surveying is rapidly growing: it is convenient, imperative, confers anonymity, attracts freer response, can be largely controlled and supervised, and speedy. Central telephone interviewing is increasing; also computer-assisted telephone interviewing (CATI) and computer interviewing (DCI).

Mail surveys are limited in effectiveness; costs should be evaluated against actual (usable) returns. Every element of mail questionnaire requires attention to ensure success.

Interviewing is a core function of marketing research; it is a social process and so interaction is important. Interviewers have four general responsibilities: (i) to locate suitable informants; (ii) to make effective interviews; (iii) to secure valid and reliable data; (iv) to record responses accurately.

Interview bias is a perennial problem; sound selection, good training and effective motivation and control help to keep this to a minimum. Qualitative research gives insight into motivations, perceptions and attitudes; it is diagnostic, and probes rather than counts. Its main techniques are group discussions, focus groups and depth interviews. Also, projective techniques are used, for example word association, sentence completion, TAT, cartoons, brainstorming.

Attitude research is important because attitudes influence everyone; three components – cognitive, affective and conative – have been identified. Scaling techniques include Likert and Semantic Differentials (Osgood).

5

Research uses

Basic techniques

The basic techniques of market research have several special applications; these have developed specific approaches with distinctive and sophisticated characteristics. Some of the principal specialized uses of market research will now be outlined.

Continuous research

Continuous research, as the title suggests, is research conducted on an ongoing basis, or is regularly repeated at frequent intervals. This type of research contrasts with *ad hoc* surveys, which are commissioned for a specific purpose and sometimes referred to as 'one-off' surveys. Popular forms of continuous or longitudinal research include consumer panels, retail audits and tracking studies.

Panels
Panels can be made up of individuals, households or firms from which comparative data from the same sampling units are taken on more than one occasion. The resultant data enable trends to be identified. Consumer purchase panels use home audits and/or diaries; many well-known research organizations involved in this specialized research, for instance, are AGB, BMRB and Research Bureau. Consumer

panel research reveals the frequency of purchase of specific products and also the extent of brand loyalty.

Panel members are selected by a systematic (quasi-random) technique or by stratified random sampling. Reporting may be weekly, quarterly or at some other agreed interval. Data may be collected via a self-completion diary or through an interviewer visiting specified homes. Clients of research companies operating these panels use the volume and expenditure data to track their comparative market performance and to evaluate, for example, the effects of promotional campaigns. Experiments may be monitored, such as different media mixes between panel areas. There have been some interesting developments with telephone panels in Capital Radio's broadcast area in London.

The AGB Attwood Consumer Panel uses a continuous sample of 4,300 households, representative of the UK population both nationally and by ITV regions in terms of age, social class, size of family and presence of children. The AGB Television Consumer Audit is based on 6,300 households who report weekly on purchases of packaged groceries. This panel will be replaced with a nation-wide panel ('Super Panel') based on 8,500 homes.

Shop audits
Regular audits of a wide range of retail stores are conducted by organizations such as A.C. Nielsen. Grocers, tobacconists, confectioners and newsagents; off-licences, pharmacies, hardware stores, DIY stores, etc., are covered in samples of stores which are audited every two months to provide information to subscribers on purchases, stocks, sales promotions and price levels. This information is vital to manufacturers; they can establish the effects of promotions, the effectiveness of distribution efforts, the 'pipe-line' position of stocks, and in-store display coverage. Sales are calculated from the following equation.

PAST STOCK + PURCHASES = PRESENT STOCK + SALES.

Sales are increasingly being computed electronically through scanning check-outs. Data provided enable market size, market trend, market share, regional demand and product availability to be continuously accessible to manufacturers to guide their marketing efforts.

Omnibus surveys
Several research agencies in the UK offer special regular surveys to clients who can insert questions and obtain data speedily. These can be

economical and effective, provided that the information sought is relatively straightforward. Different clients share this type of survey and questions can cover many aspects of marketing, such as price awareness, frequency of purchase, place of purchase and media awareness.

Most omnibus surveys are based on national samples of adults or housewives, though there are some covering specialist populations, for example car owners or regional markets. Leading agencies such as NOP, BMRB and AGB run these types of survey which are also available in some European countries.

Test marketing

Before launching products on a national scale a company may choose to try out the marketing programme in a limited way but under real-life conditions. Test marketing has been widely used by many leading fast-moving consumer goods manufacturers in order to assess people's behaviour when products are actually available to purchase. What they may have told an interviewer during a market research investigation could be contrasted with their actual behaviour at this later time.

Deficiencies in the marketing operation may become apparent and the opportunity given to rectify these shortcomings before national launch. The best combination of marketing factors (marketing mix) can be gauged from carefully studying comparative test market results over some weeks.

Test marketing cannot guarantee success. It should, however, reduce the risks involved in introducing new products (and improved versions) in highly competitive markets such as groceries and toiletries. Test markets use retail audits, consumer panels and tracking studies to check the overall patterns of demand in specific areas which are chosen to be representative of the various socio-economic groups, media coverage and distribution facilities available in a national market.

It is vital to plan carefully such test marketing: objectives should be clearly defined and criteria of success agreed; marketing operations should be fully integrated to ensure, for example, that the density of advertising and the level of sales effort are proportionate to that which may be expended on a national scale if the test gives the go-ahead.

The duration of a test marketing exercise will be largely influenced by the nature of the product surveyed, the buying frequency, the degree of competitive activity and the variable(s) being tested. This period of time may be four months or a year or more. Of course, companies may 'go national' immediately and be successful. When Rowntree-Mackintosh launched its highly successful 'Yorkie' chocolate bar the company realized that it could fairly easily be imitated, so it was decided to market this product at once throughout the London TV area. Test marketing tends to be slow, relatively expensive and, unfortunately, prone to sabotage. More recently, test marketing using computer simulated models has been developed.

Advertising research

Advertising research is a highly specialized activity of marketing research: it is concerned with the objective evaluation of advertising as a method of mass communication and persuasion. Conveniently, it can be discussed under three main headings: advertising content research, advertising media research and advertising effectiveness research.

Advertising is done by most companies, particularly in consumer product markets where huge budgets are allocated to launching new products, marketing new versions of existing products or in corporate advertising of various kinds. In 1989, advertising expenditure in the UK totalled £7,555m, of which television accounted for about one-third. The big food and household product manufacturers such as Unilever, Procter and Gamble, Kelloggs and Nestlé were among the largest spenders although they were rivalled easily by the Government for promotional campaigns covering the Training Commission, National Savings, the Treasury, etc.

The vast amounts spent on advertising indicate the serious responsibility of management to enquire systematically into its role, methods and contribution to the overall success of the firms and other organizations deeply involved in it. This assessment should include both quantitative and qualitative approaches.

Content research
Content research is concerned with studying the ability of an advertisement to achieve impact and to project the desired message to specific target customers. Every detail of a projected advertisement should be checked in a series of tests with representative audiences. Design and layout should, together, be capable of projecting an

attractive, coherent and persuasive message. Testing of advertising 'copy platform' can be at two stages: pre-publication and post-publication. With the former the focus is on gathering new ideas and methods of presentation; the latter is designed to measure what effects these planned communication concepts had on target audiences.

In 1989 Whirlpool, the US domestic appliances manufacturers, bought a 53 per cent stake ($470 million) in Philips, the Dutch electronic company's global white goods business. One of their priorities was to capitalize quickly on their investment and build a dual brand promoted on a pan-European basis. This necessitated extensive marketing research; over 1,000 women in Austria, Britain, France and Spain were individually interviewed during a systematic marketing research programme led by a French agency which coordinated research in London, Paris, Milan and Barcelona. Valuable clues were gathered, which helped in the design of a wide spread of TV campaigns introducing the dual brand of Philips/Whirlpool domestic appliances.

Advertising pre-tests

In advertising pre-tests, representative groups of individuals may view 'mock-up' advertisements (press or television) and then be subjected to a series of questions to test their recall ('noting') of specific aspects of these advertisements, for example illustration, message and action. In some cases, depth interviewing and some projective testing may take place (see previous discussion, Chapter 4). More elaborate tests may be applied to check the spontaneous emotional response to advertisements; these include physiological measurements such as the eye-blink rate and pupil dilation, galvanic skin response (popularly termed 'a lie detector') and the tachistoscope – a special slide projector which presents advertisements to viewers for very brief and gradual periods of time, often while they are questioned closely to test their ability to identify and assimilate quickly particular advertisements or, perhaps, packaging labels. Laboratory techniques are expensive and are necessarily limited in their applications.

Post-testing

Post-testing of advertisements rests on the basic techniques of recall and recognition. Tests may cover both verbal and pictorial features and may either be 'aided' (prompted) or 'unaided' (spontaneous). In the 1930s Dr George Gallup was a pioneer of these techniques in the US; Dr Daniel Starch was also active early on and developed the well-known system of 'Starch Scores' for systematically checking the detailed impact of advertisements: three measures of recognition are checked – 'noted' (percentage of readers who recalled a specific advertisement); 'seen–associated' (percentage of readers who saw or read that part of an advertisement featuring the brand name or advertiser); and 'read most' (percentage of readers who read half or more of the advertising text). Scores are ranked for all advertisements in a particular periodical and cost ratios calculated. This ingenious system may suffer from the fact that respondents may not accurately recall advertisements, perhaps confusing competitive campaigns, or be biased towards specific products because of individual interest.

Media research

Media research concentrates on objectively analysing and comparing the various media available for promoting products and services. Media owners have produced research data of increasing sophistication and reliability to support their sales campaigns to advertisers. In addition, professional organizations such as the Institute of Practitioners in Advertising (IPA) organized the *National Readership Survey* (NRS) in 1956 and since 1968 have conducted it on behalf of the Joint Industry Committee for National Readership Surveys (JICNARS), representing the Press Research Council, the IPA and the Incorporated Society of British Advertisers. This continuous survey classifies informants into social grades (A–E: see Chapter 6) and this method of socio-economic grouping, despite its critics, has become one of the best-known demographic classifications in the world. The NRS, published twice yearly, is based on a stratified random sample of 28,500 adult interviews; subscribers receive detailed information covering the major publications researched. Breakdowns are given by demographic characteristics, regional distribution, television viewing, cinema attendance, commercial radio listening, special interests and so on.

The term 'readership' has been variously defined in market research surveys, but as far as the NRS is concerned this aspect is closely defined in the introduction given to informants. Readership figures are multiples of circulation figures, which in most cases in the UK are validated by the Audit Bureau of Circulation (ABC) which issues audited statistics on a periodic basis. ABC is a professional body founded by advertisers, advertising agencies and advertising media owners in order to secure, by consistent methods of audit, accurate net sales figures for paid-for journals.

Socio-economic classification in the NRS is based on the occupation of the head of the household or chief wage-earner, which is taken as an indication of family life-style. The considerable impact of dual (and even multiple) incomes on household expenditure patterns is ignored. It assumes that people buy consistently across types of products and services; however they may, and do, spend their money disproportionately, according to personal tastes, hobbies, whims, etc.

In general the A–E groupings have served well, but they should be used with sensitivity and preferably in conjunction with other criteria (see later discussion on geodemographic systems, Chapter 6).

Television research
Television research is highly developed in the UK and is principally represented by the activities of the Broadcasters' Audience Research Board (BARB), which has covered both BBC and commercial television audience research since August 1981. BARB is responsible for commissioning both quantitative and qualitative research; the former was based on the existing system used by the Joint Industry Committee for Television Advertising Research (JICTAR), while the latter is carried out by the BBC Audience Research Department.

Techniques of television research
Originally television audiences measurement was based on electronic meters attached to TV sets in sampled households; diaries were also used. Set data are now collected by new on-line meters attached to the TV sets of a panel of 3,000 private households in the UK. Each set is monitored electronically and information passed through to a central master meter through the public telephone network.

Individual viewing is measured by push-buttons on specially designed handsets which record, electronically, individual viewing habits. These electronically based viewing panels allow longitudinal data to be collected, but they cannot guarantee that viewers are giving their sole attention to reported programmes – they may even have left the set on while asleep or out of the room.

The rapid growth in multi-set households and the increasing use of VCRs add to the complexities of television audience measurement. Multiple channels are now increasingly available with fragmentation of viewing patterns. Further technological developments will undoubtedly take place in audience measurement to keep pace with the new satellite and cable opportunities to view.

Radio research

Radio research is organized through the Joint Industry Committee for Radio Audience Research (JICRAR) which like JICNARS and JICTAR is a combined effort by the principal parties involved in advertising. Surveys are made to assess levels of listening to the various commercial radio stations and to those of the BBC. Diaries are also used in some instances.

Poster research

Poster research is conducted on a comparatively limited scale under the aegis of the Joint Industry Committee for Poster Advertising Research (JICPAR); it includes OSCAR (Outdoor Site Classification and Audience Research) – a computer bureau service which provides estimates of both pedestrian and vehicular audiences for all posters.

Cable television research

Cable television research is the focus of another joint research body known as JICCAR (Joint Industry Committee for Cable Audience Research).

Cinema research

Cinema research is included in the NRS; some other statistics on cinema attendance are given in the General Household Survey and also Social Trends.

Advertising effectiveness research

This is concerned with analysing different media (and sets of media) and evaluating the degree of success achieved against agreed advertising objectives which may be increased market share, improved public perceptions of the company. In other cases, advertising may play a defensive role, maintaining the existing market share of a product heavily under fire from competition.

Since advertising is only one element of the marketing mix (product, price, packaging, distribution, etc.) and which may be viewed from time to time, it is not easy to isolate with certainty the effects of advertising.

Under 'copy research', pre- and post-advertising techniques have been discussed. Some experimental work has been done using elaborate statistical models, though the results are generally not impressive. Computer-based simulation models are used to judge the effects of different levels of advertising expenditure across the mass media.

Other sources of advertising data

The advertising media owners publish case-studies which may be useful guides to advertising effectiveness in certain product markets; they also offer *ad hoc* and continuous research services.

The *Advertising Association* (AA) publish statistics of advertising expenditure over the UK. *Media Expenditure Analyses* (MEAL) publish, on subscription, comprehensive lists of principal advertising expenditure related to product types by companies. Monthly analyses are provided, together with the name of the advertising agency responsible for the account.

In the UK, Social Surveys (Gallup Poll) and the British Market Research Bureau (BMRB) undertake continuous surveys to check advertising effectiveness. The latter also operate Target Group Index (TGI) to provide subscribers – advertisers, agencies and media owners – with up-dated and detailed information about specific target groups of consumers and their media exposure. By using this service, advertisers can discover readily who uses their products, what they read, watch and listen to, as well as obtaining the same kinds of information related to their main competitors.

Coupon research
Coupon research is probably the oldest and simplest method of obtaining some indication of interest by readers of advertisements and, to an increasing degree, exposure to radio and television advertising.

Replies can be analysed on a cost-per-enquiry basis and different publications and media evaluated. Of course, this is a fairly crude measure of effectiveness and it would be advisable to devise follow-up enquiries, perhaps sampled on a regional basis. 'Split-run' tests (different styles of advertisement for the same product) may be inserted in the same edition of a publication and evaluation made of their comparative pulling power. Some journals run a 'readers' service' which collates advertising interest by providing readers with a readily available list of current advertisements, against which they can tick off requests for brochures, etc. While this system is useful, it may encourage the compulsive coupon-filler whose real interest in specific products is low and of little value to the advertisers concerned.

British Rate and Data (BRAD) gives detailed information on printed publications, television, radio, outdoor advertising, etc. Published monthly, this comprehensive guide includes media rates and is valuable to researchers as well as to advertsing executives.

Publishing houses and newspapers publish research data from time to time, often using independent research firms to ensure objectivity and acceptance by clients. Some of these reports are of high standard.

Industrial marketing research

The Industrial Marketing Research Association (IMRA) has defined industrial marketing as 'the systematic, objective and exhaustive search for and study of facts relevant to any problem in the field of industrial marketing'.

Nature of industrial products

Clearly, industrial products and services are of many kinds: some, for instance turbo generators or machine tools, may be exclusively used by industry whereas others, such as typewriters, insurance or stationery, may also be bought in consumer markets. However, compared with many consumer products, industrial or organizational supplies tend to be complex and sophisticated, often entailing very large sums of capital expenditure such as computer installations, power-generating plant, robot production lines, etc. Capital goods are characterized by high durability, relatively infrequent purchase, and, often, postponable demand.

Apart from capital goods, industrial supplies also include new materials, components, intermediate products such as building materials and a whole range of professional services covering financial, legal, technical and other advisory services necessary for the efficient running of a business.

Nature of industrial demand

One of the principal features of industrial markets is the nature of demand which is often directly dependent on the rate of usage of the product (or raw material, or component or sub-assembly) at later stages of demand in a specific market. This phenomenon – *derived demand* – is experienced particularly by capital equipment suppliers who are subject to investment decisions based on market expectations for the eventual product. The dependent pattern of demand for industrial raw materials is shown in Figure 5.1.

The impact of derived demand through the entire industrial pipeline emphasizes the need to study carefully trends in markets beyond these in which a company is directly active. The large fibre manufacturers, for instance, undertake market research at several levels of the fashion industry in order to understand better changing behaviour and trends in the fibre markets.

End-use analysis

End-use analysis is a particularly relevant approach to industrial market analysis. Some raw materials, such as china clay or basic chemicals, or finished products such as paint, have many applications. China clay is used not only in the pottery industry but also in the production of paper, pharmaceuticals, plastics and so on.

Analysis of the end-uses for products, components and new

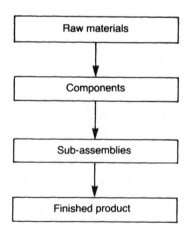

Figure 5.1 Derived demand relevant to industrial raw materials

Table 5.1 Chemical products end-use analyses

Product	Main end-use industries	
Perchlorethylene	Dry cleaning	e.g. industrial workwear rental
Ethanolamines	Detergents	e.g. household cleaners
Low density polyethylene (LDPE)	Packaging	e.g. films, sacks, shrink-wrap

materials leads to effective methods of market segmentation. Many of these market segments have distinct characteristics because of their diverse technologies and buying behaviour. Comparative analyses can be made of the market opportunities in different market sectors; some companies, such as the marine paint manufacturers, have concentrated with notable success on a significant sector which has special technical needs. Specific demand estimates can be developed from studying trends in world shipping tonnage, etc. An end-use analysis of specific chemical products is shown in Table 5.1, and which gives main end-use industries and examples of their products.

Technical advances may lead to *product substitution*, as happened with synthetic yarns largely replacing natural fibres in some market sectors. Shortages of natural raw materials have resulted in price increases which have accelerated the process of substitution.

Buying behaviour in industrial markets is markedly different from most consumer product markets; the actual number of buyers for certain products is smaller and, in some instances, there is heavy concentration of buying power over virtually monopsonistic (single buyer) presence as, for example, in coal-mining machinery or specific equipment for the nuclear industry in the UK. High concentrations of buying power are reflected in rigorous bargaining with suppliers over price, delivery, etc.

Complex decision making is another special feature of industrial markets of which researchers need to be aware when developing survey designs. Research over some years, both in the US and UK, has indicated that the buying processes involved in industrial markets tend to be lengthy, complex, and that it is not always easy to determine the precise influence exerted by those involved in the decision making process. What has been termed the *buying centre* typically covers the contributions of several executives fulfilling specific roles which have been characterized as gatekeeper, user, influencer, buyer and decider. In some cases these roles are likely to be multiple, but in many instances distinct roles can be identified according to the nature of a particular purchase consideration.

Enquiries at different levels

As far as research is concerned, this means that industrial enquiries may have to be conducted at several different levels in a company, perhaps involving design, production buying and top management. It would be vital to identify the contribution of these individuals and, in particular, to pinpoint the stage at which the eventual decisions to buy certain kinds of products are taken. Communication flows within organizations tend to be formal and informal, so some sensitive insights should be gathered when industrial surveys are being carried out. There are instances where the authority of the buyer is distinctly limited, especially in areas involving the supply of highly technical equipment. But it would be unwise to ignore his overall influence in buying decisions; his department, for example, may act as 'gatekeepers' and keep lists of approved firms who are invited to quote for specific supplies.

Nature of risk in buying

It would be useful to define industrial products by the nature of risk involved in their purchase: routine supplies such as cleaning materials or commodity products will have very different risk parameters than the purchase of high-cost fixed assets which may involve extremely large sums of money, be highly technical in nature and have long-term impact on the profitability of a business. This approach would enable market research enquiries to be focused according to the intrinsic differences in organizational supplies and the likely roles assumed by individual members of the buying centre.

Expert informants

In developing specific industrial market research approaches, it is often useful to identify recognized experts who have been connected with certain industries for many years and who may be willing to give some highly valuable clues as to the trends, both commercial and technological, which would guide research activities. Through word of mouth it is possible to locate such individuals, whose advice, based on years of experience, may enable researchers to save a great deal of effort in the early stages of designing an effective research strategy.

Techniques of industrial marketing research

As with other marketing research applications, industrial survey methodologies develop data from primary and secondary sources. Secondary data should be gathered first and, following evaluation of its coverage and contributions to the desired state of knowledge, it may be necessary to make more extensive enquiries, namely engage in primary data collection.

Secondary data sources
Secondary data sources exist both within an organization (product sales records; territory performance; customer profiles, etc.) and also externally. The latter cover statistics and reports issued by governments, trade associations, academic and technical institutions and so on.

In the UK, the Central Statistical Office (CSO) acts in a general coordinating role; the Business Statistics Office (BSO) deals specifically with industrial and commercial data. Valuable guides to data sources are *Guide to Official Statistics* (HMSO) and *Regional Statistics* (HMSO). All continental European countries operate central statistical offices; in some cases, extra data may be available on payment of a fee. (Refer to Appendix A for detailed list of secondary data sources.)

Non-official data sources are numerous in the UK: CBI Overseas Reports, Yearbooks published by Kellys, Kompass, Dun and Bradstreet, etc. are to be found in most commercial and business school libraries. Extel publishes, on subscription, details of British and European companies. The press – including *The Economist*, the *Financial Times*, the 'quality' Sunday and daily papers, contain much information of direct value to industrial market researchers.

So, as with other research activities, the first step is a thorough grounding in published data relevant to the particular industry under survey. An imaginative approach is needed as well as considerable patience in sifting out the right kinds of data, looking critically, as always, at factors which may influence their validity and reliability.

Primary data collection

Primary data collection in industrial surveys may make use of the three principal and general methods of surveying which were discussed in Chapter 4.

Observational techniques

Observational techniques may be relevant to some industrial surveys, e.g. checking the types of equipment in use and the processes involved: factors affecting safety in use may be identified and information given to guide design engineers in new product development.

Experimentation

Experimentation is necessarily restricted; the highly organized test market operations of consumer products marketing are not transferable as a whole, but it may be feasible to test alternative marketing approaches to industrial sectors and customers, perhaps through alternative methods of distribution, such as appointed stockists instead of direct sales. Different advertising media might be monitored for their effectiveness in certain market situations.

Questionnaires

Questionnaires, as customary, may be applied by personal interviewing. Industrial surveys often involve the collection of technical and scientific information, hence it is important to ensure that questions are correctly phrased and administered. It may be advisable to divide questionnaires into specific sections to be answered by, for example, financial, technical or commercial executives. This calls for considerable skill in identifying and encouraging these various respondents to participate in a survey; it also tends to increase significantly costs and the time involved in collection of data.

Telephone surveys

Telephone surveys may be particularly valuable, as noted earlier, when developing the research programme and designing an effective sampling scheme. This method is also useful when information is urgently needed. As part of the research strategy it may sometimes be advantageous to follow up selected telephone enquiries with personal interviewing in order to pursue some specific lines of enquiry of crucial importance to the objectives of a survey.

Mail surveys

Mail surveys, as already observed, may be superficially attractive but response rates are generally low, time to complete a survey is extended and real costs (which should be based on effective responses) may be high. Skill is needed to design productive mail questionnaires and, as already recommended, every aspect of this method of survey should receive detailed attention.

Personal interviewing

Personal interviewing, particularly in industrial markets, should be viewed as a task demanding special skills; these may include considerable technical background so that interviewers, who may conduct an open-style approach, are able to win the confidence of industrial and technical informants. These will clearly not be impressed by an interviewer who displays inadequate basic knowledge of their industries. In order to ensure that industrial researchers are adequately informed, a short period of basic training may be advisable. But it is important to bear in mind, however, that professional interviewing skills are of paramount importance.

Group discussions

Group discussions have been used to advantage in some industrial surveys; the qualitative data obtained as the result of open discussions with groups of engineers or other technical experts may give insights of unique value in the development of acceptable products and services.

Continuous research

Continuous research has been undertaken in industrial markets by organizations such as British Gas to develop differential pricing policies; other technically based longitudinal surveys are feasible.

Problems of sampling

Industrial or organizational markets, as discussed earlier, are often populated by very large companies or institutions and the well-known 80/20 rule applies. In forming a sample design, some general knowledge of the structure of a specific industry is crucial; this fundamental information may derive from desk research, earlier published reports or, as suggested, from discussions with expert informants.

Sampling frames

Sampling frames are sometimes difficult to acquire in industrial surveys. Many sources for these exist, for example, *Yellow Pages*, industrial and technical directories, trade associations and on-line facilities organized by data firms such as Kompass. Some specialist market research agencies may have built up highly relevant lists for certain industries and markets. The Business Statistics Office (BSO) has compiled a classified list of manufacturing businesses in the UK, and these details are available in *Business Monitor 1007* and are also available separately, for a fee, as computer print-outs related to special regional and alphabetical analysis.

Random sampling

Random sampling, as indicated in earlier discussion, is unusual in industrial market surveys: it is also unsound where markets are highly concentrated. By stratifying a specific market and taking quota samples some reasonably acceptable coverage of the population can be made. Survey findings might then be weighted according to the known or estimated sizes of the strata involved in the survey.

Industrial segmentation

In Britain, the Standard Industrial Classification (SIC – see Chapter 6) is the official basic framework for analysis of industrial and commercial activity. Industries are sub-classified on a decimal structure which allows for progressive identification of industrial segmentation. Official data are published based on these SIC identifications, and these may be valuable in developing research frameworks. In the US, the Federal Government also developed an SIC System, the basic reporting unit being the 'establishment' which may result in problems in identifying specific outputs of a multi-product establishment.

Export research

The type of information needed to market successfully overseas is similar to that required for home market operations. But because of special cultural and other environmental factors, political and legal constraints to market entry and other unfamiliar influences, market survey enquiries must be thoroughly designed.

Multi-phase approach

A systematic and sequential approach to export market research is shown in Figure 5.2. The first phase involves desk research and forms an initial screening of countries or areas which appear to offer potentially attractive opportunities for market development. Checks will be made on environmental factors; economic data such as market size, trends and possible future developments; per capita income,

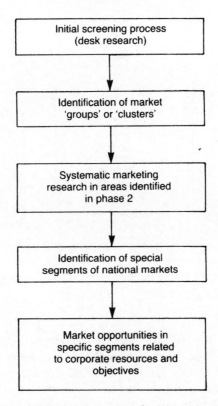

Figure 5.2 Multi-phase research for international markets

GNP, etc. From this preliminary screening, some general guides should be forthcoming as to suitable markets for cultivation.

The second phase will concentrate on researching those groups or clusters which have been identified earlier. Further studies will enable specific sectors or segments of markets to be identified; this research will be extended in succeeding phases until, finally, the data covering market opportunities will be carefully evaluated against corporate resources and objectives.

Scope of export marketing research investigations
This is illustrated in Figure 5.3, from which will be noted the comprehensive nature of the data necessary to make well-informed decisions about export business operations. Nothing should be taken for granted in overseas markets; unfamiliarity may indeed breed

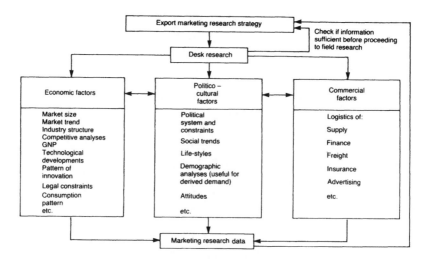

Figure 5.3   Scope of export marketing research

contempt but the results will be hazardous and even fatal for companies. Cultural norms may have profound influence on the acceptability of certain kinds of products, packaging or methods of distribution. Flavouring, consistency, colouring and labelling all affect product success. The guiding principle of a large German diversified group is: 'as much standardization as necessary, as much differentiation as possible'.

The British Standards Institution, 2 Park Street, London W1A 2BS, has a special division – Technical Help to Exporters (THE), Linford Wood, Milton Keynes, Bucks MK14 6LL, which offers advice on technical standards in European markets and also helps companies to identify foreign standards in other European markets. It publishes at regular intervals a useful technical data sheet listing standards, regulations, codes of practice and approval systems. THE also undertakes, on a consultancy basis, special investigations related to specific clients' needs.

Another source of valuable information about the European Community is to be found in Eurostat – the Statistical Office of the European Communities, which presents economic, financial, demographic, industrial and trade data on the EC member states and their trading partners. These monthly reports are obtainable from the Office for Official Publications of the European Community, or can be consulted at EC Information Centres in most European capitals and many large regional cities.

All EC member countries have national statistical offices and many of their publications are available in major libraries (see Appendix A).

Research methods
As generally practised, desk research is the first step and must be fully used before committing time and money to fieldwork. There is a wealth of data readily available from official and trade sources – for example, the British Overseas Trade Board Statistics and Market Intelligence Library, 1 Victoria Street, London SW1 (see Appendix A).

Sampling
Sampling tends to be difficult in overseas market research and it is sometimes impossible to obtain reliable sampling frames. Statistical sources in overseas countries vary considerably in their objectivity and dependability. In some countries, considerable ingenuity may be necessary in order to gather data on buying-habits and so on; free samples, small gifts and free lottery tickets have been used in some economically under-developed countries.

Formal sampling may be virtually impossible in some circumstances, although several leading UK market research agencies have overseas associates and special facilities which help to overcome problems of this nature.

Quota or convenience sampling is widely adopted in some countries, for example in Latin America.

Questionnaires
Questionnaires require expert attention not only to the subject matter but, of course, to skilful translation (which is rather different from literal translation). Multi-country enquiries obviously have special needs which Gallup, for instance, are expert in handling. They pilot such questionnaires in the UK and the revised final questionnaire is then sent to the other involved countries for translation and further piloting, if considered desirable. Translated questionnaires, together with any comments, are then returned to London where retranslation into English takes place. These are then checked against the original questionnaire and if any divergencies have occurred, corrections are made. Any changes to take account of local conditions in particular markets are made at this stage and the translations are then agreed with clients. Coding instructions, to agreed standards, are given by London to affiliate research companies. Punching and tabulation are

done in London and computer processing is controlled by London. Other leading survey firms have similar rigorous survey techniques to ensure that high-quality data results from their activities.

Principal methods of organizing research

Overseas market research can be organized in various ways, some of which are less satisfactory than others.

1. Using own staff or importing agents.
   (a) This method probably lacks objectivity; sales staff are usually unlikely to give an unbiased estimate of their products' likelihood of success.
   (b) Agents may have other interests which prevent them from giving objective assessments of the market.
   (c) Research is a specialist's job which requires particular training and experience.
   (d) This may be the only feasible method of researching in some backward markets.

2. Using research agencies in overseas markets.
   (a) Selection can be difficult and risky.
   (b) Where several markets are involved, multiple agencies may have to be used to cover the whole export programme.
   (c) A big advantage: national research organizations should possess intimate knowledge of their own home market.

3. Using a marketing research organization based in the UK plus the services of a locally based research firm.
   (a) This method is rather cumbersome and offers few advantages over method 2.
   (b) It could be useful where manufacturers had no trained research staff (often the case of smaller companies).

4. Using the services of a consortium of research agencies.
   (a) Superficially attractive, but member firms may vary considerably in the quality of their services.
   (b) An international research organization linked with advertising agencies over principal markets is usually effective.

Services research

Critical role of services

In a highly developed economy like that of the UK, radical changes have taken place in the structure of its industrial and commercial base; older industries which typified the industrial revolution have largely been supplemented by newer industries based, for example, on electronics, computer technology or sophisticated technical and advisory services.

The advanced economies of the western world now have the high proportion of their employment in the tertiary sector. The service economy is virtually a hallmark of economic development. The increasing dependence of modern economics on the efficiency of the service industries – which increasingly absorb a greater proportion of national spending power – should be a matter of direct interest to marketing specialists, including market researchers. Services increasingly support products, as with cars, industrial plant, office machinery, etc. They can add value to products – the concept of the augmented or extended product can be profitably developed on the provision of pre- and post-servicing.

The health education and welfare services add immeasurably to the well-being of the population and also to the productivity of its economic efforts. In the mixed economy of modern industrialized communities, there is an interdependence between economic and social activities as well as between industrial free enterprise firms and government-controlled services serving companies and people.

The public sector is responsible for vast sums of investment expenditure on, for example, construction of motorways, hospitals and schools. Local and regional authorities control huge budgets allocated to their various responsibilities in the purchase and provision of a wide range of goods and services: schools, libraries, welfare, recreation, planning, street cleaning, etc.

The public utility undertakings – now privatized – concerned with the supply of gas, electricity and water are large users of many products and services and in some cases, virtually the major markets for some of their suppliers.

The financial services market has expanded dynamically over the past decade or so. Most of the larger financial houses, such as the joint stock banks, building societies and insurance companies, now have marketing departments. Some have market research specialists on their staff. Leading market research agencies, such as AGB and BMRB, offer special syndicated research services to their financial clients. There is now widespread interest in financial services market research, enhanced considerably by the increasing competition now experienced in all sectors. The value of monitoring existing markets, and in research to obtain clues to new expectations, is now well accepted by banks and others who formerly stood aloof from such 'commercial' activities. New developments in financial packages are likely to emphasize the need for quality market research.

Research approach
The intangible nature of services differentiates them intrinsically from physical products, but this should not cause undue problems in research. The well-tested tools of market research are still applicable though it should be recognized that some services, such as those catering for financial or health needs, may involve sensitive matters which need to be handled with special care by trained interviewers.

Depth interviews and group discussions have been found productive in encouraging discussion on such matters. Hill Samuel used individual depth interviews with investors who had bought unit trusts over recent weeks and obtained some highly useful hints for advertising their unit trusts.

Professional market research has been used to explore the problems of hypothermia among the black, elderly unemployed in a London borough, and the provision of health and welfare services for the disabled. The Health Education Council has found market research useful in evaluating the effectiveness of poster campaigns against smoking. Research sponsored by the Department of the Environment evaluated road safety publicity particularly related to seat-belts. Results showed both a direct and positive relationship between advertising exposure and the extent of car seat-belt wearing. Of the alternative schemes surveyed, the catch-phrase 'clunk-click' appears to have been the most influential theme. Now, of course, car seat-belt wearing is legally enforced.

Community preferences in housing and environmental variables have been researched using traditional market research techniques. Social research, from whose roots market research has grown, is now one of the specialities of major research firms, apart from official surveys undertaken by government departments. Customers', clients' or patients' needs, wherever they arise, will be better served if what is offered is based on sound research into their experiences, expectations and needs.

SUMMARY

Specialized uses of marketing research are: continuous (longitudinal) research, e.g. panels, retail audits and tracking studies. Omnibus surveys and test marketing are other well-used applications.

Advertising research is a highly specialized activity of three main types: content research (pre- and post-testing), media research, and effectiveness research.

Television research (BARB) is highly developed in the UK. Other research covers radio, poster, cinema.

Effectiveness research analyses different media against agreed objectives.

Industrial marketing research uses the main techniques of marketing research but adjusted for the special nature of industrial markets, for example complexity of buying, organizational and industry structures. Derived demand and end-use analysis apply particularly to industrial marketing research enquiries.

Export marketing research emphasizes cultural and other environmental factors, political constraints and legal constraints to market entry. The range of investigations is, therefore, wide-spanning, and methods of data collection may sometimes be less formal in some overseas markets.

Services form the infrastructure of modern developed economies: their markets deserve thorough investigation if they are to serve their customers/ clients/patients well.

6

Market segmentation analyses

Role of market segmentation

Segmentation of markets enables manufacturers and distributors to design and supply products and services which appeal to particular types of buyers. Research is necessary to explore macro or total market demand and to subdivide it into significant sectors with distinctive characteristics.

Market segmentation recognizes that people differ in their tastes, needs, attitudes, motivations, life-styles, family composition and so on. It attempts to regain some of the attractive features of a small business which has close connections with its customers and knows well their individual preferences. Markets can be subdivided by several criteria; these will be influenced by the nature of the product or service, the characteristics of demand, the methods of distribution and promotion and the motivations of buyers.

Demographic analyses
Socio-economic classification has already been discussed in outline; despite its admitted drawbacks it is probably the most popular basis for consumer market segmentation. Like all analytical tools it needs to be used with discretion, particularly in conditions of social mobility and redistribution of earned incomes, etc.

NRS A–E socio-economic classification
As noted in the section on advertising research, readership surveys in the UK have been based on a socio-economic classification ranging

over six groups (A–E, as shown in Table 6.1). The NRS classifications have provided a highly useful foundation for segmentation analyses related, initially, to the readership of a wide range of publications regularly researched under the aegis of the Joint Industry Committee for National Readership Surveys (JICNARS). Other segmentation approaches have developed this basic demographic system to include family life-style, etc. (see later discussion).

The various socio-economic groups are described briefly by JICNARS as follows:

A   Upper middle class: 'the head of the household is a successful business or professional man, senior civil servant, or has considerable private means. A young man in some of these occupations who has not fully established himself may still be found in Grade "B", though he should eventually reach grade "A". In country or suburban areas, "A" grade households usually live in large detached houses or in expensive flats. In towns, they may live in expensive flats or town houses in the better parts of town'.

B   Middle class: 'In general, the heads of "B" grade households will be quite senior people but not at the very top of their profession or business. They are quite well off, but their style of life is generally respectable rather than rich or luxurious . . . non-earners will be living on private pensions or on fairly modest private means'.

C1   Lower middle class: 'in general it is made up of the families of small tradespeople and non-manual workers who carry out less important administrative, supervisory and clerical jobs, i.e. what are sometimes called "white-collar" workers'.

C2   Skilled working class: 'consists in the main of skilled manual workers and their families: the serving of an apprenticeship may be a guide to membership of this class'.

D   Semi-skilled and unskilled working class: 'consists entirely of manual workers, generally semi-skilled or unskilled'.

E   Those at lowest levels of subsistence: 'consists of old-age pensioners, widows and their families, casual workers and those who, through sickness or unemployment, are dependent on social security schemes, or have very small private means . . .'.

Table 6.1 Commercial socio-economic gradings National Readership Survey (JIC-NARS)

Social grade	Social status	Head of household's occupation	Approximate percentage of families
A	Upper middle class	Higher managerial, administrative or professional	3
B	Middle class	Intermediate managerial, administrative or professional	10
C1	Lower middle class	Supervisory or clerical and junior managerial, administrative or professional	24
C2	Skilled working class	Skilled manual workers	30
D	Working class	Semi-skilled and unskilled manual workers	25
E	Those at lowest levels of subsistence	State pensioners or widows (no other earner), casual or lowest-grade workers	8

Note: Definitions as follows.
1. A household consists of either one person living alone, or a group of persons, usually but not always members of one family, who live together and whose food and other household expenses are managed as one unit.
2. The head of household is that member of the household who either owns the accommodation or is responsible for the rent or, if the accommodation is rent-free, the person who is responsible for the household having it rent-free. If this person is a married woman whose husband is a member of the household, then the husband is counted as the 'head of the household'.
3. Chief wage earner is the senior working member of the household, normally the oldest related male of 21 years of age or over in full-time employment. If there is no male of 21 years or over then the oldest related female of 21 years and over in full-time employment is taken. Non-related persons living in the household cannot count as chief wage earners.
Source: JICNARS.

Socio-economic quotas

In Chapter 3, quota or non-probability sampling was outlined; this method is popularly used in conjunction with the A–E socio-economic classification as listed above. Typically, interviewers are given an allocation of the numbers and kinds of persons to be surveyed, specified, for example, by age, sex and social class. Proportions of the various types within the sample reflect their actual distribution in the population (refer to Table 3.2). Stratification factors may also include region, town size, etc.

Two broad types of quota control exist:

(a) independent or non-interlocking;

(b) interrelated or interlocking.

In the former case, as the description suggests, the various characteristics (age, sex, social group, etc.) are not related as, for example, in a sample of thirty informants, of whom 60 per cent, namely eighteen, were identified as women and the rest were men; or where these thirty informants are distributed among five age-groups 16–24, 25–34, 35–44, 45–64, 65+; or where the thirty informants may be classified solely by AB (13 per cent), C (54 per cent), DE (33 per cent).

Clearly, such a sample is likely to be considerably biased and could result, for example, in thirty people all of one social group being interviewed. It is preferable, and usual, to adopt the second type of quota control, namely interrelated or interlocking. Interviewers are given quotas of combined characteristics, distributed systematically over, for example, age, sex, and social group (AB men, 25–34). This avoids some of the problems associated, as observed in Chapter 4, with bias from indiscriminate selection of informants.

A quota sample of, say, 1,000 might be taken of a specific population of men and women, distributed 48 per cent male and 52 per cent female; a sample of 480 men and 520 women would thus result. If these are classified in two age groups, say X and Y (as Table 6.2), then the

Table 6.2 Example of quota control

	Age groups (%)		Total (%)
	X	Y	
Male	25	23	48
Female	27	25	52
	52	48	100

sample of 1,000 would be allocated according to the percentages of males and females in each age group.

Geodemographic classification

Some degree of dissatisfaction with the traditional A–E socio-economic classification of consumers inspired a new approach to consumer segmentation, which combines geography with demography. It is based on multivariate analysis of data derived from the UK Census of Population. Enumeration districts (EDs) are the prime geographic sources from which census data originate; each contains about 150 households which, because of their limited size, contain basically homogeneous households. In the US, the Bureau of the Census has produced detailed census data for marketing information needs for several years.

ACORN segmentation

ACORN ('A Classification of Residential Neighbourhoods') classifies people and households by types of neighbourhoods in which they live (see Tables 6.3, 6.4). With the cooperation of the Census Office the methodology was extended by CACI (the company which markets this research) and based on 1981 Census returns, eleven family groups and thirty-six neighbourhood types were distinguished, each with his own defined characteristics of age, sex, household composition, employment, joint income, family structure, type of housing, social status and car ownership (see Tables 6.3 and 6.4). The underlying logic of this sophisticated method of segmentation is that where people live frequently influences considerably their patterns of consumption, i.e. life-style. BMRB applied this thirty-six-area classification to the 24,000 respondents in their Target Group Index (TGI) survey. Profiles of particular neighbourhoods related to the consumption of food, drink, car ownership, central heating, etc., can be supplied from ACORN analyses.

Enumeration Districts (EDs) of the Census are scored 0–100, the latter figure representing the wealthiest district. 'Buying power' indices can be developed to indicate areas of high consumption of specific goods and services, such as unit trusts. ACORN has been used successfully by, for instance, building societies, banks, car manufacturers and insurance companies.

Other geodemographic systems include PiN FinPiN (financial PiN) and MOSAIC.

Table 6.3 ACORN's eleven-family group classification

ACORN groups	1981 population (000s)	(%)	Households (%)
A Agricultural areas	1811	3.4	3.3
B Modern family housing, higher incomes	8667	16.2	14.8
C Older housing of intermediate status	9420	17.6	18.7
D Poor-quality older terraced housing	2320	4.3	4.6
E Better-off council estates	6976	13.0	12.2
F Less well-off council estates	5032	9.4	10.4
G Poorest council estates	4048	7.6	6.8
H Multiracial areas	2086	3.9	3.5
I High-status non-family areas	2248	4.2	4.9
J Affluent suburban housing	8514	15.9	18.9
K Better-off retirement areas	2041	3.8	4.8
U Unclassified	388	0.7	0.1

Source: CACI International.

Life-style segmentation

'Life-style' refers to the distinctive or characteristic ways of living adopted by certain communities or segments of society. Life-styles are dynamic; people of a given occupation or income group tend to associate with each other and spend their money in characteristic ways (refer ACORN). Various ways of segmenting by life-style have been adopted; Research Bureau, a leading British marketing research agency, have developed the following groups of housewives (see Table 6.5).

ACORN life-styles list
Associated with ACORN segmentation, CACI have developed the ACORN Life-styles List which classifies every UK household into one

Table 6.4 ACORN neighbourhood types (1981)

ACORN groups			1981 population	(%)
A		Agricultural areas	1,811,485	3.4
B		Modern family housing, higher incomes	8,667,137	16.2
C		Older housing of intermediate status	9,420,477	17.6
D		Poor-quality older terraced housing	2,320,846	4.3
E		Better-off council estates	6,976,570	13.0
F		Less well-off council estates	5,032,657	9.4
G		Poorest council estates	4,048,658	7.6
H		Multiracial areas	2,086,026	3.9
I		High-status non-family areas	2,248,207	4.2
J		Affluent suburban housing	8,514,878	15.9
K		Better-off retirement areas	2,041,338	3.8
U		Unclassified	388,632	0.7
ACORN types				
A	1	Agricultural villages	1,376,427	2.6
A	2	Areas of farms and smallholdings	435,058	0.8
B	3	Cheap modern private housing	2,209,759	4.1
B	4	Recent private housing, young families	1,648,534	3.1
B	5	Modern private housing, older children	3,121,453	5.8
B	6	New detached houses, young families	1,404,893	2.6
B	7	Military bases	282,498	0.5
C	8	Mixed owner-occupied and council estates	1,880,142	3.5
C	9	Small town centres and flats above shops	2,157,360	4.0
C	10	Villages with non-farm employment	2,463,246	4.6
C	11	Older private housing, skilled workers	2,913,729	5.5
D	12	Unimproved terraces with old people	1,351,877	2.5
D	13	Pre-1914 terraces, low income families	762,266	1.4
D	14	Tenement flats lacking amenities	206,703	0.4
E	15	Council estates, well-off older workers	1,916,242	3.6
E	16	Recent council estates	1,392,961	2.6
E	17	Council estates, well-off young workers	2,615,376	4.9
E	18	Small council houses, often Scottish	1,051,991	2.0
F	19	Low rise estates in industrial towns	2,538,119	4.7
F	20	Inter-war council estates, older people	1,687,994	3.1
F	21	Council housing for the elderly	825,544	1.5
G	22	New council estates in inner cities	1,079,351	2.0
G	23	Overspill estates, high unemployment	1,723,757	3.2
G	24	Council estates with overcrowding	868,141	1.6
G	25	Council estates with worst poverty	371,409	0.7
H	26	Multi-occupied terraces, poor Asians	204,493	0.4
H	27	Owner-occupied terraces with Asians	577,871	1.1
H	28	Multi-let housing with Afro-Caribbeans	387,169	0.7
H	29	Better-off multi-ethnic areas	916,493	1.7

Table 6.4—continued

ACORN groups			1981 population	(%)
I	30	High-status areas, few children	1,129,079	2.1
I	31	Multi-let big old houses and flats	822,017	1.5
I	32	Furnished flats, mostly single people	297,111	0.6
J	33	Inter-war semis, white collar workers	3,054,032	5.7
J	34	Spacious inter-war semis, big gardens	2,676,598	5.0
J	35	Villages with wealthy older commuters	1,533,756	2.9
J	36	Detached houses, exclusive suburbs	1,250,492	2.3
K	37	Private houses, well-off elderly	1,199,703	2.2
K	38	Private flats with single pensioners	841,635	1.6
U	39	Unclassified	388,632	0.7
Area total			53,556,911	100.0

Source: CACI International.

of eighty-one life-style segments. These provide marketing management with specific targets for direct marketing strategies. ACORN Life-styles definitions are as follows:

1. Household composition.
   Singles: adults living on their own, usually without young children.
   Couples: two adults, almost certainly married, with or without young children.
   Family: two adults, almost certainly married. They have at least one other relation living with them: adult–child or other adult.
   Homesharers: multiple adults living together but not a couple or family.

2. Age structure.
   Younger: youngest – adults most often between 18 and 24 years of age. Maturing – adults most often between 25 and 44 years of age. Older: established – adults most often between 45 and 64 years of age. Retired – adults most often over 65 years of age.

In addition, analyses extend to eighty-one Life-style Types which effectively integrate consumer demographic segments and geographic locations, as Table 6.6 indicates.

83

Table 6.5   Life-style segmentation: housewives

Cluster	Definition	(%)
1	Young sophisticates Extravagant; experimental; non-traditional; young; ABC1 social class; well educated; affluent; owner-occupiers; full-time employed; interested in new products; sociable; cultural interests	15
2	Cabbages Conservative; less quality conscious; not obsessional; demographically average; more full-time housewives; middle class; average income, education; lowest level of interest in new products; very home-centred; little entertaining	12
3	Traditional working class Traditional; quality conscious; unexperimental in food; cooking enjoyed; middle-aged; DE social class; less educated; lower incomes; council house tenants; sociable; husband and wife share activities; betting	12
4	Middle-aged sophisticates Experimental, not traditional; less extravagant; middle-aged ABC1 social class; well educated; affluent; owner-occupiers; full-time housewives; interested in new products; sociable cultural interests	14
5	*Coronation Street* housewives Quality conscious; conservative; traditional and obsessional; DE social class; live relatively more in Lancashire and Yorkshire ITV areas; less educated; lower incomes; part-time employment; low level of interest in new products; not sociable	14
6	Self-confident Self-confident; quality conscious; not extravagant; young; well educated; owner-occupiers; average income; no distinctive features	13
7	Homely Bargain seekers; not self-confident; houseproud; C1C2 social class; Tyne Tees and Scotland ITV areas; left school at early age; part-time employed; average level of entertaining	10
8	Penny-pinchers Self-confident; houseproud; traditional; not quality conscious; 25–34 years; C2DE social class; part-time employment; less education; average income; betting; saving; husband and wife share activities; sociable	10

Source: Research International (RBL).

Table 6.6   Consumer demographic segmentation and geographic location

Location	Classification	(%)*
Rural areas and villages	*LA (rural singles)* LA01 Younger men LA02 Younger women LA03 Older single men LA04 Older single women LA05 Affluent singles in commuter villages LA06 Affluent singles in agricultural villages	2.7
	LB (younger rural couples and families) LB07 Young couples LB08 Young couples with elderly person LB09 Maturing couples LB10 Maturing families	2.2
	LC (older rural couples and families) LC11 Established couples LC12 Established couples, older children LC13 Retired couples LC14 Retired families	1.8
	LD (affluent rural couples and families) LD15 Affluent couples and families in commuter villages LD16 Affluent couples and families in agricultural villages	2.4
Suburbia	*LE (younger suburban singles)* LE17 Younger suburban males LE18 Younger suburban females	3.7
	LF (older suburban singles) LF19 Older single males LF20 Older single females	4.0
	LG (younger traditional suburban couples and families) LG21 Youngest couples LG22 Youngest couples with elderly person LG23 Maturing couples LG24 Maturing families	9.7
	LH (older traditional suburban couples and families) LH25 Youngest couples LH26 Established couples with older children LH27 Retired couples LH28 Retired families	5.3

Table 6.6—continued

Location	Classification	(%)*
	LI (younger very affluent suburban couples and families)	4.2
	LI29 Youngest couples	
	LI30 Youngest couples with elderly person	
	LI31 Maturing couples	
	LI32 Maturing families	
	LJ (older very affluent suburban couples and families)	2.3
	LJ33 Established couples	
	LJ34 Established families with older children	
	LJ35 Retired couples	
	LJ36 Retired families	
Council areas	*LK (younger singles in council areas)*	5.1
	LK37 Single men	
	LK38 Single women	
	LL (older singles in council areas)	5.0
	LL39 Single men	
	LL40 Single women	
	LM (younger couples in council areas)	6.8
	LM41 Youngest couples	
	LM42 Maturing couples	
	LN (older couples in council areas)	5.0
	LN43 Established couples	
	LN44 Retired couples	
	LO (adult families in council areas)	6.2
	LO45 Youngest couples and families with elderly person	
	LO46 Maturing families	
	LO47 Established families with older children	
	LO48 Retired families	
Metropolitan and cosmopolitan city	*LP (affluent single metropolitan dwellers)*	3.1
	LP49 Younger men	
	LP50 Younger women	
	LP51 Older men	
	LP52 Older women	
	LQ (affluent couples in metropolitan areas)	4.0
	LQ53 Younger couples	
	LQ54 Younger families	

Location	Classification	(%)*
	LQ55 Older couples	
	LQ56 Older families	
	LR (cosmopolitan inner city dwellers)	2.4
	LR57 Younger singles	
	LR58 Younger couples and families	
	LR59 Older singles	
	LR60 Older couples and families	
Traditional urban households	*LS (younger urban singles)*	2.8
	LS61 Men	
	LS62 Women	
	LT (older urban singles)	3.5
	LT63 Men	
	LT64 Women	
	LU (younger traditional urban couples and families)	6.8
	LU65 Youngest couples	
	LU66 Youngest couples with elderly person	
	LU67 Maturing couples	
	LU68 Maturing families	
	LV (older traditional urban couples and families)	4.3
	LV69 Established couples	
	LV70 Established families with older children	
	LV71 Retired couples	
	LV72 Retired families	
Homesharers	*LW (homesharers in affluent areas)*	3.4
	LW73 Male homesharers in very affluent areas	
	LW74 Female homesharers in very affluent areas	
	LW75 Mixed homesharers in very affluent areas	
	LW76 Male homesharers in traditional suburban areas	
	LW77 Female homesharers in traditional suburban areas	
	LW78 Mixed homesharers in traditional suburban areas	
	LX (homesharers in less affluent areas)	3.3
	LX79 Male homesharers	
	LX80 Female homesharers	
	LX81 Mixed homesharers	

*Indicates percentage of population.
Source: CAC International.

Post code

The UK post code system enables the Post Office to use mechanized sorting of mail; it is also useful for purposes of marketing research. The post code is a combination of up to seven alphabetical and numerical characters which define, in a unique way, four different levels of geographic unit (see Figure 6.1). In addition to the 22 million addresses which are post-coded, there are some very large users of mail (about 170,000) which have their own unique post-codes. On average, however, a post code contains fifteen addresses.

Post codes have many commercial applications, for example locating distribution depots; analysing advertising responses; designing sales territories. The Marketing Department of the Post Office can supply relevant back-up services, such as post coded, computerized address lists, post code maps and post code directories. The post code file has been adopted by the Office of Population and Census and is used by the National Food Survey, and also by leading marketing research organizations, such as AGB, for its home audit survey (see Chapter 5).

'SAGACITY' consumer segmentation

In 1981, Research Services developed SAGACITY, a system of segmentation combining life-cycle, income and socio-economic groups. The basic theme is that people have different aspirations and patterns of behaviour as they pass through the stages of life. Four main stages, sub-divided by income and occupation groups, are defined (see Table 6.7).

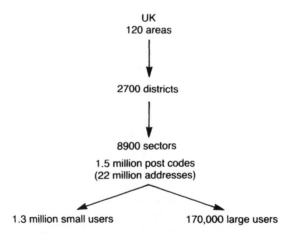

Figure 6.1 Structure of UK post code

Table 6.7 'SAGACITY' consumer segmentation

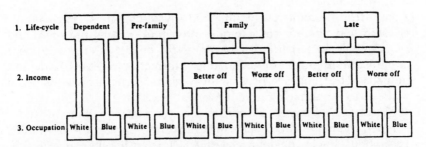

Descriptive notation has been given for each of the 12 groups, together with an indication of their size relative to the total adult population.

Dependent, white (DW) 6 per cent: Mainly under-24s, living at home or full-time student, where head of household is in an ABC1 occupation group.

Dependent, blue (DB) 9 per cent: Mainly under-24s, living at home or full-time student, where head of household is in a C2DE occupation group.

Pre-family, white (PFW) 4 per cent: Under-35s who have established their own household but have no children and where the head of household is in an ABC1 occupation group.

Pre-family, blue (PFB) 4 per cent: Under-35s who have established their own household but have no children and where the head of household is in a C2DE occupation group.

Family, better off, white (FW+) 6 per cent: Housewives and heads of household, under 65, with one or more children in the household, in the 'better off' income group and where the head of household is in an ABC1 occupation group (65 per cent are AB).

Family, better off, blue (FB+) 9 per cent: Housewives and heads of household, under 65, with one or more children in the household, in the 'better off' income group and where the head of household is in a C2DE occupation group (72 per cent are C2).

Family, worse off, white (FW−) 8 per cent: Housewives and heads of household, under 65, with one or more children in the household, in the 'worse off' income group and where the head of household is in an ABC1 occupation group (72 per cent are C1).

Family, worse off, blue (FB−) 14 per cent: Housewives and heads of household, under 65, with one or more children in the household, in the 'worse off' income group and where the head of household is in a C2DE occupation group (47 per cent are DE).

Late, better off, white (LW+) 5 per cent: Includes all adults whose children have left home or who are over 35 and childless, are in the 'better off' income group and where the head of household is in an ABC1 occupation group (60 per cent are AB).

Late, better off, blue (LB+) 7 per cent: Includes all adults whose children have left home or who are over 35 and childless, are in the 'better off' income group and where the head of household is in a C2DE occupation group (69 per cent are C2).

Late, worse off, white (LW−) 9 per cent: Includes all adults whose children have left home or who are over 35 and childless, are in the 'worse off' income group and where the head of household is in an ABC1 occupation group (71 per cent are C1).

Late, worse off, blue (LB−) 19 per cent: Includes all adults whose children have left home or who are over 35 and childless, are in the 'worse off' income group and where the head of household is in a C2DE occupation group (70 per cent are DE).

Source: Research Services Ltd.

Official British social class gradings

Registrar General: census reports

Apart from commercially inspired systems of socio-economic classification, there is considerable interest in grading the social and economic characteristics of consumers for purposes of government administration and in disseminating information to assist trade and industry. The Census Reports of the Registrar General give seventeen main socio-economic groupings (see Table 6.8).

The General Household Survey, an inter-departmental survey sponsored by the Central Statistical Office (CSO) measures, on a continuous basis, household behaviour related to factors such as housing, health, employment and education. The socio-economic groupings used are based on the first fifteen main classifications as defined by the Registrar General but these are 'collapsed' so that six classifications emerge.

The Household Food Consumption and Expenditure Survey of the Ministry of Agriculture, Fisheries and Food groups households into eight classes based on the ascertained or estimated gross income of the head of the household, or of the principal earner in the household if the weekly income of the head is less than the amount defining the upper

Table 6.8 Registrar-General's Census Report main socio-economic groupings

---

1. Employers and managers in central and local government, industry and commerce – large establishments
2. As above – small establishments
3. Professional workers – self-employed
4. Professional workers – employees
5. Intermediate non-manual workers
6. Junior non-manual workers
7. Personal service workers
8. Foremen and supervisors – manual
9. Skilled manual workers
10. Semi-skilled manual workers
11. Unskilled manual workers
12. Own account workers (other than professional)
13. Farmers – employer and manager
14. Farmers – own account
15. Agricultural workers
16. Members of armed forces
17. Indefinite

Note: In addition to the above socio-economic groupings, the Registrar General recognizes five social groups: I, II, III(N), III(M), IV and V. It will be seen that group III has been divided into N (non-manual) and M (manual).

limit of the lowest income classification (D). These main groups are as follows:

A1, A2, B, C, D, E1, E2, OAP (old-age pensioners)

From the beginning of 1980, agricultural workers, formerly in Group C, were allocated to an income group entirely on the basis of their income.

The Family Expenditure Survey of the Department of Employment bases the occupational classification used in the report on the Registrar General's socio-economic groupings, but with certain adjustments. The separate groups analysed are: professional and technical workers; clerical workers; shop assistants; manual workers and members of HM Forces. Where an individual has more than one job, the classification is related to the most remunerative occupation.

Industrial segmentation

As discussed initially in the section on industrial market research, the basic framework for analysing industrial activities in Britain is the *Standard Industrial Classification* (SIC). The revised SIC (1980) has a decimal structure comprising:

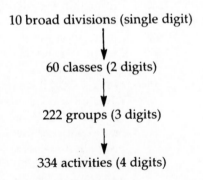

10 broad divisions (single digit)

60 classes (2 digits)

222 groups (3 digits)

334 activities (4 digits)

This progressive classification finally identifies specific industrial activities, as can be seen from the detailed lists on pages 92–108. These extracts from the *Standard Industrial Classification* (revised 1980) are reproduced with the permission of the Controller of Her Majesty's Stationery Office.

Class	Group	Activity	
			Division 0: Agriculture, forestry and fishing
01	010	0100	Agriculture and horticulture
02	020	0200	Forestry
03	030	0300	Fishing
			Division 1: Energy and water supply industries
11	111		Coal extraction and manufacture of solid fuels
		1113	Deep coal mines
		1114	Opencast coal working
		1115	Manufacture of solid fuels
12	120	1200	Coke ovens
13	130	1300	Extraction of mineral oil and natural gas
14	140		Mineral oil processing
		1401	Mineral oil refining
		1402	Other treatment of petroleum products (excluding petrochemical manufacture)
15	152	1520	Nuclear fuel production
16			Production and distribution of electricity, gas and other forms of energy
	161	1610	Production and distribution of electricity
	162	1620	Public gas supply
	163	1630	Production and distribution of other forms of energy
17	170	1700	Water supply industry
			Division 2: Extraction of minerals and ores other than fuels: manufacture of metals; mineral products and chemicals
21	210	2100	Extraction and preparation of metalliferous ores
22			Metal manufacturing
	221	2210	Iron and steel industry
	222	2220	Steel tubes
	223		Drawing, cold rolling and cold forming of steel
		2234	Drawing and manufacture of steel

Class	Group	Activity	
			wire and steel wire products
		2235	Other drawing, cold rolling and cold forming of steel
	224		Non-ferrous metals industry
		2245	Aluminium and aluminium alloys
		2246	Copper, brass and other copper alloys
		2247	Other non-ferrous metals and their alloys
23			Extraction of minerals not elsewhere specified
	231	2310	Extraction of stone, clay, sand and gravel
	233	2330	Salt extraction and refining
	239	2396	Extraction of other minerals NES
24			Manufacture of non-metallic mineral products
	241	2410	Structural clay products
	242	2420	Cement, lime and plaster
	243		Building products of concrete, cement or plaster
		2436	Ready mixed concrete
		2437	Other building products of concrete, cement or plaster
	244	2440	Asbestos goods
	245	2450	Working of stone and other non-metallic minerals not elsewhere specifed
	246	2460	Abrasive products
	247		Glass and glassware
		2471	Flat glass
		2478	Glass containers
		2479	Other glass products
	248		Refractory and ceramic goods
		2481	Refractory goods
		2489	Ceramic goods
25			Chemical industry
	251		Basic industrial chemicals
		2511	Inorganic chemicals except industrial gases
		2512	Base organic chemicals except

Class	Group	Activity	
			specialized pharmaceutical chemicals
		2513	Fertilizers
		2514	Synthetic resins and plastics materials
		2515	Synthetic rubber
		2516	Dyestuffs and pigments
	255		Paints, varnishes and printing ink
		2551	Paints, varnishes and painters' fillings
		2552	Printing ink
	256		Specialized chemical products mainly for industrial and agricultural purposes
		2562	Formulated adhesives and sealants
		2563	Chemical treatment of oils and fats
		2564	Essential oils and flavouring materials
		2565	Explosives
		2567	Miscellaneous chemical products for industrial use
		2568	Formulated pesticides
		2569	Adhesive film, cloth and foil
	257	2570	Pharmaceutical products
	258		Soap and toilet preparations
		2581	Soap and synthetic detergents
		2582	Perfumes, cosmetics and toilet preparations
	259		Specialized chemical products mainly for household and office use
		2591	Photographic materials and chemicals
		2599	Chemical products, not elsewhere specified
26	260	2600	Production of man-made fibres
			Division 3: Metal goods engineering and vehicles industries
31			Manufacture of metal goods not elsewhere specified
	311		Foundries
		3111	Ferrous metal foundries

Class	Group	Activity	
		3112	Non-ferrous metal foundries
	312	3120	Forging, pressing and stamping
	313		Bolts, nuts, etc.: springs: non-precision chains
			Metals treatment
		3137	Bolts, nuts, washers, rivets, springs and non-precision chains
		3138	Heat and surface treatment of metals, including sintering
	314	3142	Metal doors, windows, etc.
	316		Hand tools and finished metal goods
		3161	Hand tools and implements
		3162	Cutlery, spoons, forks and similar tableware: razors
		3163	Metal storage vessels (mainly non-industrial)
		3164	Packaging products of metal
		3165	Domestic heating and cooking appliances (non-electrical)
		3166	Metal furniture and safes
		3167	Domestic and similar utensils of metal
		3169	Finished metal products not elsewhere specified
32			Mechanical engineering
	320		Industrial plant and steelwork
		3204	Fabricated constructional steelwork
		3205	Boilers and process plant fabrications
	321		Agricultural machinery and tractors
		3211	Agricultural machinery
		3212	Wheeled tractors
	322		Metal-working machine tools and engineers' tools
		3221	Metal-working machine tools
		3222	Engineers' small tools
	323	3230	Textile machinery
	324		Machinery for the food, chemical and related industries, process engineering contractors
		3244	Food, drink and tobacco processing

Class	Group	Activity	
			machinery: packaging
		3245	Chemical industry machinery; furnaces and kilns; gas, water and waste treatment plant
		3246	Process engineering contractors
	325		Mining machinery, construction and mechanical handling equipment
		3251	Mining machinery
		3254	Construction and earthmoving equipment
		3255	Mechanical lifting and handling equipment
	326		Mechanical power transmission equipment
		3261	Precision chains and other mechanical power transmission equipment
		3262	Ball, needle and roller bearings
	327		Machinery for the printing, paper, wood, leather, rubber, glass and related industries; laundry and dry cleaning machinery
		3275	Machinery for working wood, rubber, plastics, leather and making paper, glass, bricks and similar materials; laundry and dry cleaning machinery
		3276	Printing, bookbinding and paper goods machinery
	328		Other machinery and mechanical equipment
		3281	Internal combustion engines (except for road vehicles, wheeled tractors primarily for agricultural purposes and aircraft) and other prime movers
		3283	Compressors and fluid power equipment
		3284	Refrigerating machinery, space heating, ventilating and air-conditioning equipment
		3285	Scales, weighing machinery and

Class	Group	Activity	
			portable power tools
		3286	Other industrial and commercial machinery
		3287	Pumps
		3288	Industrial valves
		3289	Mechanical, marine and precision engineering not elsewhere specified
	329	3290	Ordnance, small arms and ammunition
33	330		Manufacture of office machinery and data processing equipment
		3301	Office machinery
		3302	Electronic data processing equipment
34			Electrical and electronic engineering
	341	3410	Insulated wires and cables
	342	3420	Basic electrical equipment
	343		Electrical equipment for industrial use, and batteries and accumulators
		3432	Batteries and accumulators
		3433	Alarms and signalling equipment
		3434	Electrical equipment for motor vehicles, cycles and aircraft
		3435	Electrical equipment for industrial use, not elsewhere specified
	344		Telecommunication equipment, electrical measuring equipment, electronic capital goods and passive electronic components
		3441	Telegraph and telephone apparatus and equipment
		3442	Electrical instruments and control systems
		3443	Radio and electronic capital goods
		3444	Components other than active components, mainly for electronic equipment
	345		Other electronic equipment
		3452	Gramophone records and pre-recorded tapes

Class	Group	Activity	
		3453	Active components and electronic sub-assemblies
		3454	Electronic consumer goods and other electronic equipment not elsewhere specified
	346	3460	Domestic-type electric appliances
	347	3470	Electric lamps and other electric lighting equipment
	348	3480	Electrical equipment installation
35			Manufacture of motor vehicles and parts thereof
	351	3510	Motor vehicles and their engines
	352		Motor vehicle bodies, trailers and caravans
		3521	Motor vehicle bodies
		3522	Trailers and semi-trailers
		3523	Caravans
	353	3530	Motor vehicle parts
36			Manufacture of other transport equipment
	361	3610	Shipbuilding and repairing
	362	3620	Railway and tramway vehicles
	363		Cycles and motor cycles
		3633	Motor cycles and parts
		3634	Pedal cycles and parts
	364	3640	Aerospace equipment manufacturing and repairing
	365	3650	Other vehicles
37			Instrument engineering
	371	3710	Measuring, checking and precision instruments and apparatus
	372	3720	Medical and surgical equipment and orthopaedic appliances
	373		Optical precision instruments and photographic equipment
		3731	Spectacles and unmounted lenses
		3732	Optical precision instruments
		3733	Photographic and cinematographic equipment
	374	3740	Clocks, watches and other timing devices

Class	Group	Activity	
			Division 4: Other manufacturing industries
41/42			Food, drink and tobacco manufacturing industries
	411		Organic oils and fats (other than crude animal fats)
		4115	Margarine and compound cooking fats
		4116	Processing organic oils and fats (other than crude animal fat production) .
	412		Slaughtering of animals and production of meat and by-products
		4121	Slaughterhouses
		4122	Bacon curing and meat processing
		4123	Poultry slaughter and processing
		4126	Animal by-product processing
	413	4130	Preparation of milk and milk products
	414	4147	Processing of fruit and vegetables
	415	4150	Fish processing
	416	4160	Grain milling
	418	4180	Starch
	419		Bread, biscuits and flour confectionery
		4196	Bread and flour confectionery
		4197	Biscuits and crispbread
	420	4200	Sugar and sugar by-products
	421		Ice cream, cocoa, chocolate and sugar confectionery
		4213	Ice cream
		4214	Cocoa, chocolate and sugar confectionery
	422		Animal feeding stuffs
		4221	Compound animal feeds
		4222	Pet foods and non-compound animal feeds
	423	4239	Miscellaneous foods
	424	4240	Spirit distilling and compounding
	426	4261	Wines, cider and perry
	427	4270	Brewing and malting
	428	4283	Soft drinks

Class	Group	Activity	
	429	4290	Tobacco industry
43			Textile industry
	431	4310	Woollen and worsted industry
	432		Cotton and silk industries
		4321	Spinning and doubling on the cotton system
		4332	Weaving of cotton, silk and man-made fibres
	433	4336	Throwing, texturing, etc. of continuous filament yarn
	434	4340	Spinning and weaving of flax, hemp and ramie
	435	4350	Jute and polypropylene yarns and fabrics
	436		Hosiery and other knitted goods
		4363	Hosiery and other weft knitted goods and fabrics
		4364	Warp knitted fabrics
	437	4370	Textile finishing
	438		Carpets and other textile floor coverings
		4384	Pile carpets, carpeting and rugs
		4385	Other carpets, carpeting, rugs and matting
	439		Miscellaneous textiles
		4395	Lace
		4396	Rope, twine and net
		4398	Narrow fabrics
		4399	Other miscellaneous textiles
44			Manufacture of leather and leather goods
	441	4410	Leather (tanning and dressing) and fellmongery
	442	4420	Leather goods
45			Footwear and clothing industries
	451	4510	Footwear
	453		Clothing, hats and gloves
		4531	Weatherproof outerwear
		4532	Men's and boys' tailored outerwear
		4533	Women's and girls' tailored outerwear

Class	Group	Activity	
		4534	Work clothing and men's and boys' jeans
		4535	Men's and boys' shirts, underwear and nightwear
		4536	Women's and girls' light outer-wear, lingerie and infants' wear
		4537	Hats, caps and millinery
		4538	Gloves
		4539	Other dress industries
	455		Household textiles and other made-up textiles
		4555	Soft furnishings
		4556	Canvas goods, sacks and other made-up textiles
		4557	Household textiles
	456	4560	Fur goods
46			Timber and wooden furniture industries
	461	4610	Sawmilling, planing, etc. of wood
	462	4620	Manufacture of semi-finished wood products and further processing and treatment of wood
	463	4630	Builders' carpentry and joinery
	464	4640	Wooden containers
	465	4650	Other wooden articles (except furniture)
	466		Articles of cork and plaiting materials, brushes and brooms
		4663	Brushes and brooms
		4664	Articles of cork and basketware, wickerwork and other plaiting materials
	467		Wooden and upholstered furniture and shop and office fittings
		4671	Wooden and upholstered furniture
		4672	Shop and office fitting
47			Manufacture of paper and paper products Printing and publishing
	471	4710	Pulp, paper and board
	472		Conversion of paper and board

Class	Group	Activity	
		4721	Wall coverings
		4722	Household and personal hygiene products of paper
		4723	Stationery
		4724	Packaging products of paper and pulp
		4725	Packaging products of board
		4728	Other paper and board products
	475		Printing and publishing
		4751	Printing and publishing of newspapers
		4752	Printing and publishing of periodicals
		4753	Printing and publishing of books
		4754	Other printing and publishing
48			Processing of rubber and plastics
	481		Rubber products
		4811	Rubber tyres and inner tubes
		4812	Other rubber products
	482	4820	Retreading and specialist repairing of rubber tyres
	483		Processing of plastics
		4831	Plastic-coated textile fabric
		4832	Plastics semi-manufactures
		4833	Plastics floorcoverings
		4834	Plastics building products
		4835	Plastics packaging products
		4836	Plastics products not elsewhere specified
49			Other manufacturing industries
	491	4910	Jewellery and coins
	492	4920	Musical instruments
	493	4930	Photographic and cinematographic processing laboratories
	494		Toys and sports goods
		4941	Toys and games
		4942	Sports goods
	495		Miscellaneous manufacturing industries
		4954	Miscellaneous stationers' goods
		4959	Other manufactures not elsewhere

Class	Group	Activity	
			specified
			Division 5: Construction
50			Construction
	500	5000	General construction and demolition work
	501	5010	Construction and repair of buildings
	502	5020	Civil engineering
	503	5030	Installation of fixtures and fittings
	504	5040	Building completion work
			Division 6: Distribution, hotels and catering; repairs
61			Wholesale distribution (except dealing in scrap and waste materials)
	611	6110	Wholesale distribution of agricultural raw materials, live animals, textile raw materials and semi-manufactures
	612	6120	Wholesale distribution of fuels, ores, metals and industrial materials
	613	6130	Wholesale distribution of timber and building materials
	614		Wholesale distribution of machinery, industrial equipment and vehicles
		6148	Wholesale distribution of motor vehicles and parts and accessories
		6149	Wholesale distribution of machinery, industrial equipment and transport equipment other than motor vehicles
	615	6150	Wholesale distribution of household goods, hardware and ironmongery
	616	6160	Wholesale distribution of textiles, clothing, footwear and leather goods
	617	6170	Wholesale distribution of food, drink and tobacco
	618	6180	Wholesale distribution of pharmaceutical, medical and other chemists' goods
	619	6190	Other wholesale distribution including general wholesalers
62			Dealing in scrap and waste materials
	621	6210	Dealing in scrap metals

Class	Group	Activity	
	622	6220	Dealing in other scrap materials or general dealers
63	630	6300	Commission agents
64/65			Retail distribution
	641	6410	Food retailing
	642	6420	Confectioners, tobacconists and newsagents; off-licences
	643	6430	Dispensing and other chemists
	645	6450	Retail distribution of clothing
	646	6460	Retail distribution of footwear and leather goods
	647	6470	Retail distribution of furnishing fabrics and household textiles
	648	6480	Retail distribution of household goods, hardware and ironmongery
	651	6510	Retail distribution of motor vehicles and parts
	652	6520	Filling stations (motor fuel and lubricants)
	653	6530	Retail distribution of books, stationery and office supplies
	654	6540	Other specialized retail distribution (non-food)
	656	6560	Mixed retail businesses
66			Hotels and catering
	661		Restaurants, snack bars, cafés and other eating-places
		6611	Eating-places supplying food for consumption on the premises
		6612	Take-away food shops
	662	6620	Public houses and bars
	663	6630	Night clubs and licensed clubs
	664	6640	Canteens and messes
	665	6650	Hotel trade
	667	6670	Other tourist or short-stay accommodation
67			Repair of consumer goods and vehicles
	671	6710	Repair and servicing of motor vehicles
	672	6720	Repair of footwear and leather goods
	673	6730	Repair of other consumer goods

Class	Group	Activity	
			Division 7: Transport and communication
71	710	7100	Railways
72			Other inland transport
	721	7210	Scheduled road passenger transport and urban railways
	722	7220	Other road passenger transport
	723	7230	Road haulage
	726	7260	Transport not elsewhere specified
74	740	7400	Sea transport
75	750	7500	Air transport
76			Supporting services to transport
	761	7610	Supporting services to inland transport
	763	7630	Supporting services to sea transport
	764	7640	Supporting services to air transport
77	770	7700	Miscellaneous transport services and storage not elsewhere specified
79	790		Postal services and telecommunications
		7901	Postal services
		7902	Telecommunications
			Division 8: Banking, finance, insurance, business services and leasing
81			Banking and finance
	814	8140	Banking and bill-discounting
	815	8150	Other financial institutions
82	820	8200	Insurance, except for compulsory social security
83			Business services
	831	8310	Activities auxiliary to banking and finance
	832	8320	Activities auxiliary to insurance
	834	8340	House and estate agents
	835	8350	Legal services
	836	8360	Accountants, auditors, tax experts
	837	8370	Professional and technical services not elsewhere specified
	838	8380	Advertising
	839		Business services

Class	Group	Activity	
		8394	Computer services
		8395	Business services, not elsewhere specified
		8396	Central offices not allocable elsewhere
84			Renting of movables
	841	8410	Hiring out agricultural and horticultural equipment
	842	8420	Hiring out construction machinery and equipment
	843	8430	Hiring out office machinery and furniture
	846	8460	Hiring out consumer goods
	848	8480	Hiring out transport equipment
	849	8490	Hiring out other movables
85	850	8500	Owning and dealing in real estate
			Division 9: Other services
91			Public administration, national defence and compulsory social security
	911		National and local government services not elsewhere specified
		9111	National government service not elsewhere specified
		9112	Local government service not elsewhere specified
	912	9120	Justice
	913	9130	Police
	914	9140	Fire services
	915	9150	National defence
	919	9130	Social security
92			Sanitary services
	921		Refuse disposal, sanitation and similar services
		9211	Refuse disposal, street cleaning, fumigation, etc.
		9212	Sewage disposal
	923	9230	Cleaning services
93			Education
	931	9310	Higher education
	932	9320	School education (nursery, primary

Class	Group	Activity	
			and secondary)
	933	9330	Education not elsewhere specified and vocational training
	936	9360	Driving and flying schools
94	940	9400	Research and development
95			Medical and other health services: veterinary services
	951	9510	Hospitals, nursing homes, etc.
	952	9520	Other medical care institutions
	953	9530	Medical practices
	954	9540	Dental practices
	955	9550	Agency and private midwives, nurses, etc.
	956	9560	Veterinary practices and animal hospitals
96			Other services provided to the general public
	961	9611	Social welfare, charitable and community services
	963	9631	Trade unions, business and professional associations
	966	9660	Religious organizations and similar associations
	969	9690	Tourist offices and other community services
97			Recreational services and other cultural services
	971	9711	Film production, distribution and exhibition
	974	9741	Radio and television services, theatres, etc.
	976	9760	Authors, music composers and other own account artists not elsewhere specified
	977	9770	Libraries, museums, art galleries, etc.
	979	9791	Sport and other recreational services
98			Personal services
	981		Laundries, dyers and dry cleaners
		9811	Laundries
		9812	Dry cleaning and allied services
	982	9820	Hairdressing and beauty parlours

Class	Group	Activity	
	989	9890	Personal services not elsewhere specified
99	990	9900	Domestic services
00	000	0000	Diplomatic representation, international organizations, allied armed forces

Until 1980, when the present classification was devised, SICs were divided into Minimum List Headings (MIHs) which, while generally useful, often failed to result in sufficiently specific product classifications; care is still needed, however, in interpreting data from sources using the SIC; for example, because the unit of classification is the establishment which is not necessarily identical with a particular company's overall trading activities.

Examples of industrial market segmentation are given in Figures 6.2 and 6.3 and Table 6.9. From Figure 6.2 it will be noted that coiled extendable electrical leads have four main end-use markets. Taking the domestic end-uses as an example, the many applications of this product will readily be seen, and demand for the electrical leads will obviously be affected by the rate of purchase of the appliances listed.

Table 6.9 illustrates the user segments of the fire protection market. There are sub-segments related to the nature of the hazard for which the equipment is designed, and also the kinds of fire-extinguishing systems for which these products are used. This systematic market analysis reflects thoroughly the need to research in depth macro markets and to obtain relevant data.

Table 6.9 UK industrial fire protection market user segments

	Fire-extinguishing systems			
	Sprinklers	Deluge	Halon	Foam
Special hazard				
Power stations	x	x	x	x
Oil and gas		x	x	x
Petrochemicals		x	x	x
Ordinary hazard				
Manufacturing	x	x	x	
Distribution	x		x	
Public sector			x	

Note: In addition, there are specialized marine applications.

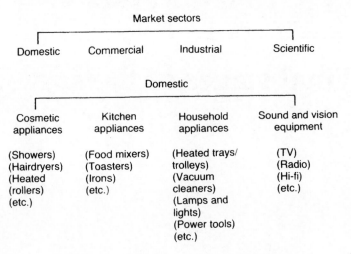

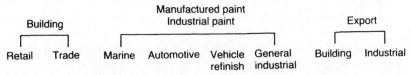

Figure 6.2   Coiled extendable electrical leads

Figure 6.3   Usage segmentation of paint market

Figure 6.3 gives a user segmentation of the paint market, which has two principal sectors in the home market, namely building and industrial, plus an important export sector. These sectors are further divided into highly specific end-use markets.

SUMMARY

Market segmentation analyses underlie successful marketing performance. Research is necessary to identify specific significant sectors so that products/ services can be developed and marketed to meet these needs. Segmentation can be of many kinds: demographic (NRS A–E socio-economic groups); geodemographic (ACORN, MOSAIC, etc.); Life-Style; 'Sagacity', etc. Official British Social Classifications vary over ministries, and there is need for some harmonization.

Industrial segmentation is officially based on the Standard Industrial Classification (SIC).

7

Final stages of the survey

Data processing tasks

The sequential tasks in the process of market research (as given in Figure 3.1, Chapter 3) will have resulted in intimidating quantities of questionnaires and other documents containing the raw data. Processing is the next task; this includes *editing* of survey forms, *coding* of answers (if not pre-coded) and *tabulation*.

Editing
Every question should be checked to see either that it has been answered or, if not, that it was not applicable to the particular respondent. If there is missing information critical to the survey's findings, interviewers may be asked to call back and collect it or, perhaps, it may be feasible to complete the questionnaire by telephoning the respondent. To avoid problems of this nature at a late stage in the survey, it would be advisable to check survey forms at regular intervals, so that any call-backs may be done conveniently by field staff who are still in the neighbourhood.

Editing demands vigilance and patience; obvious inaccuracies, some of which may be facetious or extremely doubtful, should be rejected. Surveys often include 'check' questions to test the validity of other responses. The consistency and accuracy of the responses over the entire questionnaire are checked during this important phase of the research process.

Coding

After editing, the next task is the coding of answers for analytical purposes. Questionnaires are usually printed with coding so that interviewers can complete these during interviews. From pilot testing of the questionnaire, it will have been possible to enter sets of alternative coded responses on the final questionnaire.

Open questions call for different treatment; after examining a representative selection of completed survey forms, experienced research staff draw up categories with which answers can be allocated and coded. Clearly, a questionnaire with many open questions is going to impose considerable demands on research time and skills. Code categories should be mutually exclusive and relevant to the purposes of the survey.

In the case of CATI and DCI techniques (see Chapter 4), a direct input of coded responses is made by telephone interviews with the former system or by respondents in the latter case.

Tabulation

Following editing and coding, tabulation occurs; this prepares quantitative data in an understandable form, such as counting the frequency of certain cases in a given classification.

Tabulation can be either manual, mechanical or electronic; the appropriateness of a method will depend on the nature of the survey and the speed with which the findings are needed. Generally, a simple survey, perhaps of no more than 500 questionnaires, could be hand processed. This becomes difficult – if not impossible – when cross-tabulations are complex or lengthy. At one time, the Hollerith system of punched cards was widely used in market research data processing, but has been largely replaced by mainframe and micro-computers. There are special market research software packages suitable for micros; spreadsheets are widely adopted and are of varying levels of sophistication.

Computers handle complex data so speedily and seductively that there is the danger of 'data indigestion'; of being drowned in data. Discretion should be used as to the quality and quantity of the data inputs to avoid what has been dubbed 'the GIGO syndrome' (garbage in – garbage out).

Data have to be organized systematically before they can be processed by computer using, as noted, suitable software packages. The Statistical Package for the Social Sciences (SPSS) is one of the best-known computer packages. Also, the Economic and Social Research Council (ESRC) maintains a register of software packages suitable for market and social surveys. Specialist agencies offer data processing services in most cities and large towns in the UK.

In considering the analyses required for specific surveys, the following points should be borne in mind:

1. What statistical measures are going to be used in the report data? Simple statistical descriptions as averages, percentages, distributions and measures of dispersion are generally adopted. Will these be adequate for the objectives of a particular survey?

2. What cross-tabulations are likely to be helpful to clients? For example, socio-economic groupings by marital status related to ownership of some consumer durable. Researchers should check carefully the kinds of cross-tabulations required and ensure that the specific computer package will be capable of delivering these.

Data may be examined to detect possible relationships; it is customary, for example, to explore whether a positive or negative correlation exists between product use and type of industry or, as in the case of life assurance, between adoption and socio-economic groups. Care should be exercised in interpreting correlations. Correlation merely indicates the degree of movement between two (or more, in the case of multiple regression) variables; it is a measure of association but the existence of correlation does not imply that the relationship is necessarily causal. Data should be selectively handled; there is no point in cramming a report with masses of data which have only peripheral value to a client.

Reliability of data should be stated by researchers. It is customary for tests of significance to be quoted; these indicate the degree to which certain statistical measures may be accepted. However, the results of significance tests are valid only for the particular samples taken in a survey; other samples (of different size) may reveal data that react differently to a test of significance.

Hence, sweeping assertions based on tests of significance should be avoided. Even though a survey finding may be statistically 'significant', the degree of magnitude of the statistic may be so limited that it is likely to have very little substantive interest. Clearly, apart from statistical expertise, common sense is required in the evaluation of survey data. As observed earlier, according to the complexity and volume of the data collected tabulations and analyses may range from hand-processing to sophisticated computer packages. But it is useless – if not decidedly dangerous – to apply sophisticated statistical tests to data which originate from an unsound research design. Unless care is taken at every stage of the survey process, the resultant information, masquerading as scientific, may be worth less than subjective opinion.

Preparation and presentation of survey report

Analysis and evaluation of data transform the raw data collected during the field survey (and from desk research) into management information. This now has to be communicated in an attractive and effective manner.

Guidelines to report
The following points will guide this process:

1. The style of the report should relate to the needs of clients. It may be desirable, for example, to have two (or more) editions of a report; one with detailed technical data for technical specialists, the other, principally for commercial management, might cover technology at less depth but concentrate more on the commercial implications of survey findings. If only one edition is planned, technical terms should be carefully defined, perhaps in an appendix.

2. Clear grammatical language should be used in survey reports.

3. Diagrams and tables used in survey reports should be captioned, units of measurement clearly quoted and, if published material is used, the source should be given.

4. It is largely a matter of expediency and taste whether textual matter should be interspersed with diagrams and tables. Extracts from lengthy tables may be given in the text of a report, and the complete data presented in an appendix.

5. The type of printing and binding of survey reports should be checked with researchers. Also, the number of copies of survey reports which will be submitted to clients should be checked.

6. Clients often find it helpful for researchers to make a formal presentation of the main findings of a survey at a meeting of senior executives. This matter should be checked with researchers before the research is commissioned. Copies of the survey report should preferably be distributed before such a meeting so that executives

have the opportunity of raising matters arising from scrutiny of research findings.

7. This final stage of the research process involves professional skills in communication. Both the content and style of the report should satisfy the needs of specific clients. The format, printing and binding of the report deserve considerable care; they help to make a report intelligible and effective. Whether researchers should inter- pret the research findings is open to debate; some clients are content with the facts being reported, while others seek for the researchers' interpretations because it is likely that they will have acquired special insight into the business and its markets. The scope of researchers' responsibilities should, of course, be clarified in the research proposal.

8. Research reports should present survey findings within a logical framework. Although particular surveys will have specific head- ings, the general outline scheme on page 115 is suggested.

Buying market research
'Make or buy' decisions frequently have to be made by industrial management; this principle can apply to services as well as products. Many companies rely on professional advice from outside their organization in matters of law, finance, taxation, design, etc. Their own staff may be qualified in these disciplines but are likely to act more as general practitioners than specialists. When expert knowledge at some depth is required, outside help may be sought. Therefore, companies may decide to supply from their own resources a certain level of marketing research, but seek to augment their needs through research agencies as and when research becomes more sophisticated or large scale.

Those companies seeking outside suppliers of marketing research should, first of all, carefully identify their marketing problems and specify the types of data they wish to have. This exercise will form a useful base for discussions with prospective research agencies.

Independent marketing research companies tend to be either (i) those offering a comprehensive range of services or (ii) those specializ- ing by function or by type of research undertaken. The larger agencies, such as AGB or BMRB, offer broadly based experience in all aspects of survey practice. Smaller agencies often specialize in particular kinds of enquiry, for example psychological testing or services such as ques- tionnaire construction or interviewing. Large specialist agencies such

114

Typical profile of market report

Title page

Contents page

List of appendices

Text of report
> Introduction (purpose of report)
> Main conclusions (series of short statements)
> Methodology (outline of research)
> Details of survey methodology
> Survey findings (text plus tables and diagrams)
>> Definition of product market
>>> Domestic production
>>> Imports
>>> Market trends
> Target market size
> Planned market share
>> Nature of buying behaviour
>> Nature of competition
>> Prices
>> Promotion
>> Distribution
>> Packaging
>> After-sales service
>> Delivery
> Summary of survey findings
General conclusions and recommendations

List of tables

List of diagrams

References

Appendices

as Nielsen's undertake a continuous audit of selected retail outlets (see Chapter 5). In addition to commercial research firms, several academic institutions have been able to provide professional assistance to companies with marketing problems of many kinds. The British Institute of Management, the Chartered Institute of Marketing, the Market Research Society and the Industrial Marketing Research Association can supply lists of members who are qualified to offer suitable services.

Consultation with trade associations and past and present clients of research agencies may also help in identifying and selecting suitable research agencies, who could be invited to submit details of their services with particular reference to the needs of the enquirer.

Selected agencies could then be asked to prepare an outline proposal together with costs; the eventual supplier would require to be fully briefed by the client company (see Chapter 3). An executive member of the client's staff should be nominated to work closely with the research company during the survey.

Interpreting and using marketing research findings

When the survey has been completed and the resultant data collected and analysed, the question of the interpretation of the survey findings arises. Should the research agency's responsibilities extend to interpreting the data, or should they be asked merely to present these data? Clients should clarify these matters, so that both they and their researchers work well together. Full value should be derived from the unique insight which researchers have gained into clients and their markets, so it would seem advantageous to encourage them to reinforce the data by soundly based interpretation relevant to the specific markets that have been investigated.

Costing marketing research

Methods of evaluating the costs and benefits of marketing research range from subjective estimates to sophisticated decision theory based on Bayesian decision rules. At the simplest level, the toss of a coin might be used to decide whether or not to enter a particular market, e.g. a 50/50 chance of success might relate to a market launch of £250,000. But the more novel the product and dynamic the market environment, the greater the risk in making decisions on this basis.

Existing information might, however, result in a 60/40 chance of success. In this case, the estimated cost of a wrong decision would be computed thus:

$$£250,000 \times 40\% = £100,000$$

If more and better information could be obtained through marketing research, the chances of success might be 80/20, and this would mean that on the launch figure quoted above, the estimated loss would be about £50,000 if market entry failed. Hence, the value of marketing research would be calculated as follows:

£100,000 (wrong decision − £50,000 (wrong decision = £50,000
 taken with present information, i.e. 60/40 basis) taken with extra information, i.e. 80/20 basis)

Hence, up to £50,000 could be usefully spent on marketing research in order to enhance the chances of market success.

A more sophisticated approach to evaluating research expenditure would involve Bayesian decision theory which uses the concepts of utility, subjective probabilities and Bayes' theorem for revision of prior judgements of hypotheses. The theory tends to be rather complex and is detailed in statistical textbooks, but the following simplified example indicates the essential nature of Bayesian analysis applied to marketing research evaluation.

A company wishes to expand into a new market and has been told that detailed marketing research investigation would cost about £50,000. Prior analysis of this marketing venture allows them to estimate the probability of attaining a market share of at least 15 per cent at 0.6:

	Market share > 15%		Market share <15%	
	Probability	Payoff	Probability	Payoff
Enter market	0.6	£300,000	0.4	(£50,000)
Do not enter market	0.6	0	0.4	0

Expected Monetary Value (EMV) is one of the most suitable criteria that could be adopted for evaluating this project, although there are others which might also be applied. Hence:

EMV = 0.6 (£300,000) + 0.4 (−£50,000) = £160,000

If posterior analysis is now applied, it may be assumed that this product is already on sale in another market. Information on existing sales performance indicates that earlier predictions of 75 per cent success were actually realized. Taking this increased probability into account, the revised EMV can be calculated as follows:

$$\text{EMV}_2 = 0.75 \, (\pounds300,000) + 0.25 \, (-\pounds50,000) = \pounds212,500$$

The value of the additional information is calculated thus:

$$\text{EMV}_2 - \text{EMV}_1$$
$$= \pounds212,500 - \pounds160,000$$
$$= \pounds52,500$$

A marketing survey costing £30,000 could, therefore, be afforded. It would appear worth while to reduce the level of uncertainty regarding market entry, provided that research findings could be available without a long delay.

Although Bayesian decision theory applies probabilities and results in fairly imposing mathematical equations, the probabilities are derived from estimates and are subjective in nature. The elegance of the theory should not be allowed to obscure its inherent fragility. So far this technique does not appear to be widely used in evaluating marketing research estimates. Generally, however, decisions to undertake marketing research appear to be based more on pragmatism than sophisticated costing appraisals.

Data protection
The UK was comparatively late in adopting data protection legislation: implementation in the UK was effected by the Data Protection Act which became law on 12 July 1984. The Act is concerned with *individuals*, not corporate bodies; it does not refer to the processing of personal data by manual means.

The market research industry has generally favoured some form of data protection legislation. It has had Codes of Practice for more than thirty years. The MRS Code of Practice is still stronger with regard to protecting personal data than the Data Protection Act. Some organizations operate, of course, outside of the MRS and the Association of Market Survey Organizations (AMSO) and do not follow these codes, but similar codes have now been established for the European Society for Opinions and Marketing Research (ESOMAR) and the International Chamber of Commerce. Useful guides to the Data Protection Act are available from the Office of the Data Protection Registrar, Spring-field House, Water Lane, Wilmslow, Cheshire SK9 5AX.

SUMMARY

Data processing involves three stages: editing, coding and tabulation. All phases require skilful attention.

Computers can handle complex data speedily but care should be exercised to avoid 'data indigestion'; also beware of the GIGO syndrome.

Reports should be expertly planned and be relevant to the information needs of clients. They should be clearly written, effectively illustrated with tables, diagrams, etc. Printing and binding deserve special care.

Costing the benefits of marketing research can lead to fairly abstruse calculations; common sense is needed as well as computational skills.

The requirements of the Data Protection Act should be borne in mind when handling computerized data.

Appendix A: Desk research notes

Only rarely is there no existing and relevant information about a particular research problem; internal records or published statistics are often capable of giving remarkably useful information which may be sufficient for the decisions which have to be taken. Desk research is the vital first step in developing the overall research strategy (refer to Figure 2.2, Chapter 2).

Secondary data – internal

As discussed in Chapter 3, the answers to many problems often lie within the files of an organization or in published material. The internal records of a company – production, costing, sales and distribution – should be designed so that the information they contain could also be useful for marketing research purposes. Sales analysis should be designed to give information by markets, products, types of distributive outlet or industry, geographic area (home and overseas) and characteristics of customers, such as heavy/medium/light buyers. Advertising expenditure should be carefully recorded and analysed by media, product type and market. Other promotional expenses should also be available for market researchers to study. Some internal data may not be readily available and considerable checking of invoices may be necessary to establish product sales. If this is likely to be an extremely difficult task, some estimates may have to be made based on factory production figures for particular periods.

Secondary data – external

External sources of data include statistics and reports issued by governments, trade associations and other reputable organizations. Research companies and advertising agencies frequently circulate useful information. Further information is obtainable from trade directories.

In the UK, the Government Statistical Service offers detailed data of great value to marketing researchers. Two very useful official publications are *Guide to Official Statistics* (HMSO) and *Regional Statistics* (HMSO).

The Central Statistical Office (CSO), Great George Street, London SW1, or The Business Statistics Office (BSO), Cardiff Road, Newport, Gwent, would give advice on the availability of statistical data for particular types of products and markets. The CSO also publish annually a useful booklet, *Government Statistics: a Brief Guide to Sources*, which lists the various ministries and departments (with telephone numbers) responsible for specific economic and social data, for example the *Annual Statistics in Retail Trades*, or the *Classified List of Manufacturing Businesses* – this publication, which is available in special regional and alphabetical analyses at reasonable cost – is useful in building up a specific industry mailing list or sampling frame.

Some other principal sources of official information are listed below:

Annual Abstract of Statistics: provides information on population, housing, manufactured goods, etc.

Monthly Digest of Statistics: similar to above but published at monthly intervals.

Abstract of Regional Statistics: main economic and social statistics for regions of the UK.

Scottish Abstract of Statistics: main statistics for Scotland.

Digest of Welsh Statistics: main statistics for Wales.

Economic Trends: monthly review of economic situation.

Social Trends: collection of key social statistics (yearly).

Digest of Health Statistics for England and Wales (yearly).

Agricultural Statistics: England and Wales (yearly).

Financial Statistics: key UK monetary and financial statistics (monthly).

Digest of Energy Statistics (yearly).

Highway Statistics (yearly).

Passenger Transport in Great Britain (yearly).

Housing and Construction Statistics (quarterly).

Monthly Bulletin of Construction Statistics.

Overseas Trade Statistics of the UK (monthly).

Family Expenditure Survey Reports (yearly).

National Income and Expenditure 'Blue Book' (yearly).

Census of Production: conducted since the beginning of this century at approximately five-yearly intervals.

Census of Population: full census every ten years.

Annual Estimates of the Population of England and Wales and of Local Authority Areas (yearly).

Census of Distribution: last full-scale census in 1971 provided basic information on structure of retail areas of distribution; from 1976 superseded by annual sample enquiries.

Department of Employment Gazette (monthly).

Department of Trade and Industry: *British Business* (formerly *Trade and Industry Journal*) (weekly).

Bill of Entry Service: Customs and Excise data.

Business Monitors: detailed information about many important industries in the UK.

Several of the official sources of data mentioned above are particularly significant in industrial and export marketing research.

Non-official sources of data in the UK are plentiful and are published by trade associations, banks, academic institutions, the trade and professional press and national newspapers, as well as survey reports by commercial research firms. Very useful guides are *Sources of UK Marketing Information* by Elizabeth Tupper and Gordon Wills (Benn, 1975) and, more briefly, *Principal Sources of Marketing Information* by Christine Hull (Times Newspapers).

Another very comprehensive source of data was published in 1979 by John Wiley: *Where to find business information* lists over 5,000 main sources and comments on them in some detail. Some specific sources of market data are given below.

National press

The Economist; Financial Times; The Times; Daily Telegraph; The Guardian; The Independent; Sunday Times; Observer, etc.

Official publications

British Business, formerly titled the *Trade and Industry Journal*, is published by the Department of Trade and Industry, and is a valuable source of information about industrial and commercial trends both at home and overseas. Also publishes industry reviews, statistical data and news about trade fairs and overseas missions.

Trade press and technical

Specialist journals cover almost every major industry and trade; some cater for highly specific segments. Typical examples are: *The Grocer; Chemist and Druggist; Packaging News; The Bookseller; Motor Trader; Applied Ergonomics; Footwear International* (details can be found in *Willing's Press Guide* and *British Rate and Data Guide* (BRAD).

Subscription services

Mintel Market Intelligence Reports, published monthly, with useful cumulated index at end of each new issue; mostly concerned with consumer products. Mintel also publish a quarterly *Retail Intelligence* and some special major studies of various market sectors.

Mintel Digest 1992 monitors every UK national paper, selection of international papers, and over 100 trade journals.

ADMAP: monthly journal giving information and statistical data covering all advertising media with special thrice-yearly analyses of advertising expenditures by product categories and media.

Media Expenditure Analysis (MEAL): monitors advertising expenditure across all media types. Publishes quarterly in *MEAL Digest* detailed information related to product brands and individual advertisers.

The Economist Group, partly under the name The Economist Intelligence Unit (EIU), publishes on a regular basis reports on certain industrial sectors, e.g. the automotive industry, retail distribution, etc. as well as special reports on topics of current interest.

Retail Business and *Marketing in Europe*, published monthly, give valuable coverage of specific aspects of markets; a series of printed indexes enable past data to be readily tracked and trends evaluated.

As a result of a management buy-out in 1984, *The Corporate Intelligence Group* was formed; this publishes *ad hoc* surveys for clients, and also continuing surveys on off-highway equipment and industries in North America and West Europe.

Euromonitor publish *Market Research Great Britain* (monthly) and *Market Research Europe* (bi-monthly); coverage given of up to ten fairly specific topics per issue, e.g. mineral water or television market in Spain.

BLA Group publish *Market Assessment* (bi-monthly) covering home, office and leisure market sectors in the UK; often useful for industrial market analysis.

Financial Times Business Information Service, established in 1971, provides a broadly based impartial business intelligence service covering all aspects of national and international industry and commerce. Detailed information can include brand shares, advertising expenditures, production, import, export and sales figures for most industries. Demographic analyses of purchasing or usage patterns are available. Special project investigations can also be undertaken. The FT Business Information Service has close links with FINTEL, jointly owned by the FT and Extel to develop electronic information services; it is the major provider of business information in PRESTEL, the UK Post Office viewdata system.

CBI Overseas Reports issued quarterly by Confederation of British Industries.

NEDO Reports (National Economic Development Office): publish reports on a range of industries.

Special financial analyses

Extel Group publish details of British and European companies.

Jordans Industrial and Financial Surveys: although principally focus on providing ratios for comparative purposes in particular market sectors, these reports also include useful overviews and reviews of specific industrial structures and trends.

ICC Business Ratio Reports also gives specific information related to ratios of corporate efficiency.

Keynotes Reports cover about 200 consumer and industrial market sectors, giving market size and trends, financial data, industrial structure, etc. Recent press articles on these specific markets are listed.

Gower Press; valuable series of economic surveys covering several industries/markets.

TV audience reports

Available from individual television contractors and also specialist research agencies.

Yearbooks and Directories

Kelly's *Kompass Register*: *Kelly's Directory of Manufacturers and Merchants;* Dun and Bradstreet's directories: *Guide to Key British Enterprises; International Market Guide; British Middle Market Directory; Who Owns Whom.*

Times Top 1000 lists major British-based companies.

Advertisers Annual (IPC) lists media, suppliers of advertising and promotional services, advertising agencies and principal advertisers listed geographically.

Retail Directory (Newman) lists stores and other distributive outlets.

Benn's Press Directory, in two volumes, gives details of printed media, e.g. regional newspapers.

BRAD (British Rate and Data) gives detailed information on newspapers, magazines, television, radio, the cinema, outdoor advertising and other media. Published monthly, this media guide is invaluable to researchers, advertising executives, etc.

Croner Publications Detailed and regularly up-dated business information covering commercial law, business strategy, EC data, etc.

Market Research Society Yearbook Published by the Market Research Society (MRS); this reference book contains a list of members, a detailed list of organizations providing market research services and the Code of Conduct.

International Directory of Market Research Organisations, jointly sponsored by the MRS and the British Overseas Trade Board (BOTB); lists 1,500 market research organizations in sixty-seven countries, plus names and addresses of all major national market research associations.

On-line Services
Pergamon Infoline has more than twenty databases covering marketing and sales prospecting, finance and credit checking, business intelligence and news and British Trademarks and British Standards.

Kompass On-line, based on the well-known Kompass hard-copy directories, covering over 23,000 companies in Europe. Provides company name and address, telephone/telex numbers, description of business, number of employees, named executives and, where feasible, sales figures.

On-line Patents Search
The Search and Advisory Service
The Patent Office
Room 312 State House   (moving to Newport,
66–71 High Holborn   South Wales, in 1991)
London WC1R 4TP

Will undertake extensive, specialized searches in patent literature with national and international coverage. New product concepts can be checked against international technical trends and commercial developments.

Professional institutions, etc.

Association of Market Survey Organisations (AMSO)
Ince House
60 Kenilworth Road
Leamington Spa
CV32 6JY

(AMSO accounts for about two-thirds of all commercially available UK research activities).

British Institute of Management (BIM)
Africa House
64–78 Kingsway
London WC2B 6BL

Confederation of British Industry (CBI)
21 Tothill Street
London SW1

Industrial Marketing Research Association (IMRA)
11 Bird Street
Lichfield
Staffordshire

Chartered Institute of Marketing
Moor Hall
Cookham
Berkshire SL6 9QH

Institute of Practitioners in Advertising (IPA)
Belgrave Square
London SW1X 8QS

Advertising Association
Abford House
15 Wilton Road
London SW1V 1NJ

Market Research Society
15 Northburgh Street
London EC1

Among its publications are *MRS Newsletter* and *MRS Survey* giving up to date information about market research courses and seminars, and also features on market research techniques and developments.

National Institute of Economic and Social Research
2 Dean Tench Street
London SW1

Barclays Bank Group
Economic Intelligence Unit
54 Lombard St
London EC3

Lloyds Bank
Overseas Department
6 Eastcheap
London EC3

Association for Information Management (ASLIB)
26–27 Boswell Street
London WC1N 3JZ
(Authoritative source of diverse range of information)

In addition, some of the larger Chambers of Commerce, e.g. London, Birmingham and Manchester, may be able to provide very useful data related to specific industries. Local authorities, particularly the larger ones, may also be able to provide industrial and commercial data for their areas. Another useful source could be organizations which promote industry in specific regions; New Town Development Corporations, etc.

Companies House may also be relevant for certain types of enquiries; some leading firms of stockbrokers may have undertaken research into specific industries.

Leading commercial libraries

City Business Library
London EC2

Science Reference Library
Chancery Lane
London WC2

Statistics and Market Intelligence Library
1 Victoria Street
London SW1

London Business School Library

Manchester Business School Library Information Service

Warwick University Library Business Information Service publish monthly, on a subscription basis, *Market and Statistic News*, which contains a review of business information, on-line news, statistical features, etc.

Civic Commercial Libraries.

Overseas governments issue statistics and reports of use to marketing researchers. Some sources tend to be more reliable than others, and experienced researchers evaluate the information obtainable. Some of the larger research organizations, e.g. Nielsen or Gallup, have overseas companies or associates which can provide accurate data in specific market areas.

As already mentioned, exploitation of all reliable sources of data during desk research should be the first step in marketing research. In some cases the information resulting from persistent and patient desk research may be sufficient for management's needs.

Appendix B: Examples of questionnaires

These questionnaires provide useful examples of questionnaire construction and cover a variety of market investigations which clearly illustrate the wide applicability of marketing research surveys.

Arts sponsorship survey

Self-completion questionnaire, subsequently coded, which focuses on firms' interest in sponsorship of the arts.

Note that the questionnaire contains guidance to respondents who give alternative answers.

Manchester International Airport – car parking survey

Highly structured and fully coded questionnaire administered by group of interviewers to airport travellers and visitors.

Running a car and car accessories survey

Example of self-completion questionnaire to find out car users' attitudes and buying behaviour.

Note that questions 6 and 7, for example, contain discrete classfications of mileage or age of car.

Hotel accommodation survey

Structured questionnaire personally administered to discover hotel guests' feelings and experiences related to hotel accommodation, service, etc.

Question 1 was designed to relax respondents but it was, perhaps, slightly biased. However, the general approach and scope of the questionnaire is well disciplined.

Oxfam shoppers' survey

Questionnaire, administered by team of interviewers, to discover attitudes and behaviour of Oxfam shoppers (note use of scales).

Two towns were involved: the commuter town of Knutsford and an old industrial town, Oldham (question 2 was obviously modified).

Sponsorship of the arts

Questionnaire

---

1   Many industries today are looking at alternative avenues for 'promoting' their businesses, and are becoming more aware of 'sponsorship' as a vehicle for this. Have you as a company ever been involved in sponsorship (excluding any political contributions) of any kind?

Please tick.

YES   ☐

NO   ☐

If *No* go to question 8.

---

2   Are you currently involved in any form of sponsorship?

Please tick.

YES   ☐

NO   ☐

3 If you answered *Yes* to question 2, which of the following describe(s) the sponsorship you undertook?

Please tick.

Education	☐
Sport	☐
Charity	☐
The 'Arts'	☐

---

4 What was the main reason for entering into sponsorship?

Please tick.

As part of general promotional strategy ☐

Public relations exercise/corporate image ☐

Strong personal interest of senior member

of the company ☐

Other. Please specify _____

_____

---

5 What level of sponsorship have you allocated to particular sponsorship events in 1983 and 1984? In the table below use a separate column for each event and allocate the level of expenditure accordingly.

Please tick.

Number of events

£	1	2	3	4	5 or more
0–499					
500–999					
1,000–4,999					
5,000–10,000					
over 10,000					

6   Which of the following methods of sponsorship did you use in 1983 and 1984?

Please tick.

Covenants   ☐

Direct payments   ☐

Gifts in kind   ☐

Joint promotional activities   ☐

Promotional literature   ☐

Other. Please specify _____

_____

7   In undertaking sponsorship, companies sometimes take advantage of tax concessions. Did your company utilize any of the following?

Please tick.

By deed of covenant   ☐

Secondments of staff with salary paid by the company   ☐

Gifts of kind directly related to the products/
services marketed by the company   ☐

Advertising, in promotional literature for an event   ☐

8   Companies sometimes make use of sponsorship schemes. Are you aware of any of the following?

Please tick.

Tax advantages of sponsorship   ☐

The Government Business Sponsorship Incentive Scheme   ☐

The Association of Business Sponsorship   ☐

---

9   Are you considering sponsorship in the future?

Please tick.

YES   ☐

NO   ☐

MAYBE   ☐

---

10   Various companies have been involved in sponsorship of the arts. In your opinion what do you think motivated these companies to utilize Arts sponsorship?

Please tick.

As part of general promotional strategy   ☐

Public relations exercise/corporate image   ☐

Strong personal interest of senior member of the company ☐

---

11   Do any of the following types of art appear suitable to you as a medium for sponsorship?

Please tick.

Painting/sculpture *classical*   ☐

Painting/sculpture by living artists *contemporary*   ☐

Films   ☐

Theatre   ☐

Music   ☐

None of the above   ☐

---

12   Do you think that sponsorship of the contemporary arts would be useful to your company in any of the following ways?

Please tick.

Promoting particular products   ☐

Promoting company image   ☐

Public relations activity   ☐

---

13   Does your company own a piece of *Contemporary* Art?

Please tick.

YES   ☐

NO   ☐

DON'T KNOW ☐

---

14   Would your company be interested in acquiring a piece of *Contemporary* Art for display, e.g. in the reception area, Board room?

Please tick.

	Purchase	Loan
YES	☐	☐
NO	☐	☐
MAYBE	☐	☐

---

15   Would your company be interested in purchasing a piece of *Contemporary* Art specifically commissioned for your company?

Please tick.

YES   ☐

NO   ☐

MAYBE   ☐

If *No* please go to question 17.

---

16   About how much would your company be prepared to pay for such a commissioned piece of work?

£

Up to 99	☐
100–499	☐
500–999	☐
1,000–5,000	☐
Over 5,000	☐

---

17 Would your company be interested in utilizing the resources of a small art gallery able to accommodate up to 100 people for special business meetings, promotions, etc.?

Please tick.

YES ☐

NO ☐

MAYBE ☐

---

18 What facilities would you expect to be available?

Please tick.

Audio-visual equipment ☐

Display facilities ☐

Refreshments ☐

Other. Please specify _____

_____

---

19 If you have any further comments you would like to make in connection with your company's attitude to sponsorship of the *Contemporary Arts*, please use the space below to make them.

Manchester International Airport – car parking survey

Questionnaire

1 | Is this the first time you have been to the airport?
IF 'NO' ASK:

2 | How many times have you been to the airport in the last 12 months?

0	[1]	
1	[2]	
2–6	[3]	1
7+	[4]	☐

3 | Which of the following is your reason for being here today?

FLIGHT PASSENGER	[1]
MEETING SOMEONE	[2]
SEEING SOMEONE OFF	[3]
SIGHTSEEING	[4]

2
☐

4 | Are you on a visit to this country or a permanent resident in the UK?

Visitor	[1]	3
UK resident	[2]	☐

Questionnaire for deplaning passengers

5 | *ASK OR OBSERVE*

Scheduled domestic	[1]	
Scheduled international	[2]	4
Charter international	[3]	☐

6 | What was the reason for your trip?

> PRIVATE BUSINESS [1]
> COMPANY BUSINESS [2]
> HOLIDAY [3]
> VISITING FRIENDS AND RELATIONS [4]

5

☐

7 | How long have you been away?

Less than 24 hours [1]   8–14 days [4]

24–48 hours [2]   More than 14 days [5]

Up to 7 days [3]   I'm arriving [6]

ASK [8] ONLY IF [6] HERE OTHERWISE [9]

6

☐

8 | How long are you staying?

Less than 24 hours [1]   8–14 days [4]

24–48 hours [2]   More than 14 days [5]

Up to 7 days [3]

7

☐

9 | What transport will you use to leave the airport?

Private car [1]   Private coach [4]

Hire car [2]   Public transport [5]

Taxi [3]   Other [6]

8

☐

Appendix B

---

10 | *IF 'PUBLIC TRANSPORT'*

Have you any particular reason for using public transport?
Have you another reason?

Live near bus route	[1]	Left car for family use	[6]
No car	[2]	Cheapness	[7]
Don't like leaving car	[3]	Efficient service	[8]
Cost of car parking	[4]	Other	[9]
Travelling with	[5]		
several friends			

9

☐

1st
reason

IF NOT 'PUBLIC TRANSPORT'
Have you any particular reason for not using public transport?
Have you another reason?

Don't live near bus route	[1]	Luggage problems	[6]
Comfort/privacy	[2]	Cost	[7]
Speed/time	[3]	Unreliable/timing	[8]
Changing is complicated	[4]	Inclusive package tour	[9]
Unaware of availability	[5]		

10

☐

2nd
reason

---

11 | About how far have you got to go?

Less than 10 miles	[1]	41–60 miles	[4]
10–20 miles	[2]	61–100 miles	[5]
21–40 miles	[3]	Over 100 miles	[6]

11

☐

---

12 | And where are you travelling to?
*ELICIT RESPONSE AND REFERRING TO TOWN LIST,
DETERMINE ACCURATE RESPONSE*

12 13
☐☐

IF ANSWER 'I'M ARRIVING AT [7] *TERMINATE NOW*

UNLESS ANSWER 'PRIVATE CAR' AT [9] *TERMINATE NOW*

13 | What transport did you use to get to the airport on your outward flight?

Private car	1	Private coach	4		
Hire car	2	Public transport	5	14	
Taxi	3	Other	6	☐	

14 | *IF 'PUBLIC TRANSPORT'*
Have you any particular reason for using public transport?
Have you another reason?

Live near bus route	1	Left car for family use	6
No car	2	Cheapness	7
Don't like leaving car	3	Efficient service	8
Cost of car parking	4	Other	9
Travelling with several friends	5		

15

☐

1st
reason

IF NOT 'PUBLIC TRANSPORT'
Have you any particular reason for not using public transport?

Don't live near bus route	1	Luggage problems	6
Comfort/privacy	2	Cost	7
Speed/time	3	Unreliable/timing	8
Changing is complicated	4	Inclusive package tour	9
Unaware of availability	5		

16

☐

2nd
reason

15 | Are you a driver yourself?   Yes   1   17
IF 'NO' TERMINATE NOW   No   2   ☐

16 | Where was the vehicle parked?

Multistorey	1	Surface Park G	4
Surface Park C	2	Other	5
Surface Park F	3	Not parked/dropped off	6

IF 5 *OR* 6 *HERE TERMINATE NOW*

18

☐

17 | How long was the cark parked?

Up to 30 mins	1	1–2 days	8
Up to 1 hour	2	2–3 days	9
Up to 2 hours	3	3–4 days	10
Up to 3 hours	4	4–5 days	11
Up to 4 hours	5	5–6 days	12
Up to 12 hours	6	Up to 7 days	13
Up to 24 hours	7	Up to 14 days	14

19 20

☐ ☐

18 | How much do you think that would cost?

ENTER FIGURE, e.g. 0 0 5 0

21 22   23 24

☐☐ ☐☐

19 | Do you expect car park prices to go up in the next year?

Definitely Yes	1	No	4
Yes	2	Definitely No	5
Don't know	3		

ASK 20 *ONLY IF* 1 *OR* 2 *HERE OTHERWISE* 21

25

☐

20	How much do you think they would go up? *ENTER FIGURE AS BEFORE*	26 27 28 29 ☐☐ ☐☐

21	*SHOW CARD WITH PRESENT AND FUTURE FIGS. EXPLAIN:* Please would you indicate which car park price would stop you bringing the car and come by some other means?	30 31 ☐☐

PLEASE TERMINATE NOW, GO TO END AND COMPLETE
DATE AND IDENTIFICATION CODES

Questionnaire for enplaning passengers

22	*ASK OR OBSERVE*
	    Scheduled domestic 1
	    Scheduled international 2
	    Charter international 3
		32
		☐

23	What is the reason for your trip today?
	
	    PRIVATE BUSINESS 1
	    COMPANY BUSINESS 2
	    HOLIDAY 3
	    VISITING FRIENDS AND RELATIONS 4
		33
		☐

24	How long will you be away? Less than 24 hours 1 8–14 days 4 24–48 hours 2 More than 14 days 5 Up to 7 days 3 I'm returning 6 *ASK* 25 *ONLY IF* 6 *HERE OTHERWISE* 26	34 ☐

---

25 How long have you been here?

Less than 24 hours	[1]	8–14 days	[4]	
24–48 hours	[2]	More than 14 days	[5]	35
Up to 7 days	[3]			☐

---

26 What transport did you use to get to the airport?

Private car	[1]	Private coach	[4]	
Hire car	[2]	Public transport	[5]	36
Taxi	[3]	Other	[6]	☐

---

27 IF 'PUBLIC TRANSPORT'

Have you any particular reason for using public transport?
Have you another reason?

Live near bus route	[1]	Left car for family use	[6]	
No car	[2]	Cheapness	[7]	
Don't like leaving car	[3]	Efficient service	[8]	37
Cost of car parking	[4]	Other	[9]	☐
Travelling with several friends	[5]			1st reason

IF NOT 'PUBLIC TRANSPORT'
Have you any particular reason for not using public transport?
Have you another reason?

38
☐
2nd reason

Don't live near bus route	[1]	Luggage problems	[6]	
Comfort/privacy	[2]	Cost	[7]	
Speed/time	[3]	Unreliable/timing	[8]	
Changing is complicated	[4]	Inclusive package tour	[9]	
Unaware of availability	[5]			

28	How far did you have to come?				
	Less than 10 miles	1	41–60 miles	4	
	10–20 miles	2	61–100 miles	5	39
	21–40 miles	3	Over 100 miles	6	□

29	And where have you come from? *ELICIT RESPONSE AND REFERRING TO TOWN LIST. DETERMINE ACCURATE RESPONSE*	40 41 □ □
	IF 'I'M RETURNING' AT 24 *TERMINATE NOW*	
	UNLESS 'PRIVATE CAR' AT 26 *TERMINATE NOW*	

30	Are you a driver yourself?	Yes 1	42
	IF 'NO' TERMINATE NOW	No 2	□

31	Where is the vehicle parked?				
	Multistorey	1	Surface Park G	4	
	Surface Park C	2	Other	5	43
	Surface Park F	3	Not parked/dropped off	6	□
	IF 5 *OR* 6 *HERE TERMINATE NOW*				

32	How long is the car parked for?				
	Up to 30 mins	1	1–2 days	8	
	Up to 1 hour	2	2–3 days	9	
	Up to 2 hours	3	3–4 days	10	
	Up to 3 hours	4	4–5 days	11	
	Up to 4 hours	5	5–6 days	12	44 45
	Up to 12 hours	6	Up to 7 days	13	□ □
	Up to 24 hours	7	Up to 14 days	14	

145

33 | How much do you think that would cost?

ENTER FIGURE, e.g. | 0 | 0 | 5 | 0 |

46 47 48 49

34 | Do you expect car park prices to go up in the next year?

Definitely Yes	1	No	4
Yes	2	Definitely No	5
Don't know	3		

74

ASK 35 ONLY IF 1 *OR* 2 *HERE. OTHERWISE* 21

35 | How much do you think they would go up?
ENTER FIGURE AS BEFORE

75 76 77 78

36 | *SHOW CARD WITH PRESENT AND FUTURE FIGURES,*
EXPLAIN:
Please would you indicate which car park price would stop you
bringing the car and come by some other means?

79

*PLEASE TERMINATE NOW, GO TO END AND COMPLETE DATE
AND IDENTIFICATION CODES.*

Questionnaire for meeters and greeters

37 | What transport did you use to get to the Airport?

Private car	1	Private coach	4
Hire car	2	Public transport	5
Taxi	3	Other	6

50

38 *IF 'PUBLIC TRANSPORT'*
a) Have you any particular reason for using public transport?
b) Have you another reason?

Live near bus route	1	Left car for family use	6
No car	2	Cheapness	7
Don't like leaving car	3	Efficient service	8
Cost of car parking	4	Other	9
Travelling with several friends	5		

51

☐

1st reason

IF NOT *'PUBLIC TRANSPORT'*
a) Have you any particular reason for not using public transport?
b) Have you another reason?

Don't live near bus route	1	Luggage problems	6
Comfort/privacy	2	Cost	7
Speed/time	3	Unreliable/timing	8
Changing is complicated	4	Inclusive package tour	9
Unaware of availability	5		

52

☐

2nd reason

39 *IF MEETER*
About how far have you got to travel from the Airport?
IF SEEING OFF
About how far have you travelled to get to the Airport?

Less than 10 miles	1	41–60 miles	4
10–20 miles	2	61–100 miles	5
21–40 miles	3	Over 100 miles	6

53

☐

40 *IF MEETER*
Where are you going to?
IF SEEING OFF
Where have you come from?
ELICIT RESPONSE AND REFERRING TO TOWN LIST,
DETERMINE ACCURATE RESPONSE

54 55

☐☐

147

UNLESS 'PRIVATE CAR' AT [34] *TERMINATE NOW*

41	Are you a driver yourself?	Yes [1]	56
	IF 'NO' TERMINATE NOW	No [2]	☐

42	Did you drive the car yourself?	Yes [1]	57
		No [2]	☐

---

43 | Where is the vehicle parked?

Multistorey	[1]	Surface Park G	[4]
Surface Park C	[2]	Other	[5]
Surface Park F	[3]	Not parked/dropped off	[6]

58 ☐

IF [5] *OR* [6] *HERE TERMINATE NOW*

---

44 | How long will the vehicle be parked?

Up to 30 mins	[1]	1–2 days	[8]
Up to 1 hour	[2]	2–3 days	[9]
Up to 2 hours	[3]	3–4 days	[10]
Up to 3 hours	[4]	4–5 days	[11]
Up to 4 hours	[5]	5–6 days	[12]
Up to 12 hours	[6]	Up to 7 days	[13]
Up to 24 hours	[7]	Up to 14 days	[14]

59 60 ☐☐

---

45 | About how much do you think that will cost?

ENTER FIGURE, e.g. [0][0][5][0]

61 62   63 64
☐☐ ☐☐

46	Do you expect car park prices to go up in the next year?

Definitely Yes   1   No   4

Yes   2   Definitely No   5

Don't know   3

ASK 44 *ONLY IF* 1 *OR* 2 *HERE, OTHERWISE* 45

65
☐

---

47   How much do you think they would go up?
ENTER FIGURE AS BEFORE

66 67   68 69
☐☐   ☐☐

---

48   *IF SEEING OFF*
Please would you indicate which car park price would stop you bringing people to the Airport

SHOW CARD WITH PRESENT AND FUTURE PRICES AND EXPLAIN

70
☐

IF MEETING
Please would you indicate which car park price would stop you coming to collect passengers from the Airport
SHOW CARD WITH PRESENT AND FUTURE PRICES AND EXPLAIN

PLEASE TERMINATE NOW
COMPLETE DATE AND IDENTIFICATION CODES

DATE NO.

71 72
☐☐

73
☐

INTERVIEWER

Manchester University Business School Survey

Number of Cars
in Household ☐

Running a car survey

Notes on how to complete this questionnaire

- Please place a tick √ in the appropriate box
- Do not write in the right hand margin
- Please answer for one car only throughout this questionnaire

PLEASE DO NOT
WRITE HERE

1.	I am	1. Male	☐	☐	1.
		2. Female	☐		
2.	I am aged	1. 17–24	☐		
		2. 25–34	☐		
		3. 35–44	☐	☐	2.
		4. 45–54	☐		
		5. 55–64	☐		
		6. 65+	☐		
3.	Who is the owner of the car?	1. Private	☐		
		2. Company	☐	☐	3.
	(One car only, please)				
4.	Where was the car bought?	1. Local	☐		
		2. Greater Manchester	☐	☐	4.
		3. Outside Greater Manchester	☐		

Appendix B

5. What is the make of the car? (e.g. Ford, Toyota)
Please specify: _____ □□ 5/6.

6. Approximately how many miles did you drive
last year (1980)?

    1.   Less than 5,000 □

    2.   5,001–10,000 □

    3. 10,001–15,000 □

    4. 15,001–20,000 □   □ 7.

    5. 20,001–25,000 □

    6. Over 25,000 □

7. How old is the car?

    1. Less than 12 months □

    2. Between 1–2 years □

    3. Between 2–3 years □

    4. Between 3–4 years □   □ 8.

    5. Between 4–6 years □

    6. Between 6–8 years □

    7. Between 8–10 years □

    8. Over 10 years □

8. How many miles, to the nearest 1,000, has the car travelled
(as registered on the clock)?

Please specify: _____ □ 9/10.

151

Appendix B

9. The maintenance of the car is normally carried out by:

    Either (a) the garage where the car was bought ☐

    or   (b) other garage(s) ☐

    or   (c) another person (outside the household) ☐   ☐ 11.

    or   (d) myself/someone else in the household ☐

10. The *parts* are normally provided by:

    Either (a) the garage from where the car was bought ☐

    or   (b) other garage(s) ☐   ☐ 12.

    or   (c) another person (outside the household) ☐

    or   (d) myself/someone else in the household ☐

11. If you have bought any of the following parts or accessories in
    the last 12 months, please tick the appropriate box.
    (*You may tick more than one*):

    (a) Simple accessories. ☐   ☐ 13.
        Examples only: driving gloves, anoraks,
                        steering wheel covers,
                        petrol cans, etc.

    (b) Other minor accessories and parts. ☐   ☐ 14.
        Examples only: spark plugs, interior or
                        exterior special trim (clocks,
                        radios, dashboard extras,
                        external fancy stickers, etc.),
                        light bulbs, spotlights,
                        fanbelts, air filters, etc.

    (c) Parts for minor repairs – electrical and ☐   ☐ 15.
        mechanical

    (d) Parts for major repairs – electrical, bodywork, ☐   ☐ 16.
        mechanical

12. Please indicate where you bought parts and accessories in the last 12 months.

	Which (name)	Where (town)
A. A garage		
B. Mail order		
C. A motor parts and accessories shop		
D. Other shop		
E. Second-hand		
F. Other		

☐ 17.

☐ 18.

☐ 19.

☐ 20.

☐ 21.

☐ 22.

13. Please list as many reasons as you can for your choice of source, as indicated in Question 12. Here is an *example*:

Source	(Example only)	Reasons (example only)
C.	It is close by, has helpful staff, etc.	
B.	It is well known, easy to use, etc.	

Source	Reasons

14. Please indicate *in order of preference* the features which you would
     expect to find if a 'perfect' car parts and accessories 'super-
     market' existed within a few miles of your home.

A. Discount prices	1st	□ 23.
B. Good parking facilities	2nd	□ 24.
C. Wide range of goods	3rd	□ 25.
D. Good quality	4th	□ 26.
E. Well-trained staff	5th	□ 27.
F. Easy to get to	6th	□ 28.
G. Long opening hours	7th	□ 29.
H. Any other reason	8th	□ 30.
(please state below)		

15. We would welcome any further comments either about this
     questionnaire or about matters relating to this questionnaire.
     (Please use the space below and, if necessary, on the back.)

THANK YOU

The market for hotel accommodation

Hotel Guest Questionnaire

HOTEL
CODE

I am from Manchester University, carrying out a survey on the market for hotel accommodation. Could you spare me a few minutes to answer some questions about your experiences?

☐ 1

☐ 2

Q1 I have heard that some people find hotels rather boring and sometimes even lonely places. What are your feelings about hotels?

(Record answer) ....

▨ 3

....

....

....

....

Q2 If you had had the choice, would you have preferred to stay:

(1) With friends
(2) With relatives
(3) In a hotel

☐ 4

Q3 Would you say that, on the whole, hotels give good value for money?

(1) Yes   (2) No

(Record comments) ....

☐ 5

....

....

....

Q4 How did you first get to hear about this particular hotel?

    (1) Friends or relatives   (5) Hotel's own booking agency
    (2) Travel agent   (6) Other booking agency
    (3) Hotel's advertising   (7) Other
    (4) A hotel guide

    If 'other' please state: ....

    ....

    ....

    ....

(1) ☐	6
(2) ☐	7
(3) ☐	8
(4) ☐	9
(5) ☐	10
(6) ☐	11
(7) ☐	12

Q5 Many factors could be involved in choosing a hotel, but if you had to pick the one factor that was most important to you in choosing this hotel, what would it be?

    (1) Facilities   (5) Near target destination
    (2) Price   (6) Near travel terminus
    (3) Been before   (7) Other
    (4) Recommended

    If 'other' please state: ....

    ....

☐ 13
☐ 14

Q6 The next question is a little more abstract, so please base your answers on a general impression rather than pure fact.
(GIVE CARDS) On each page of the booklet here is a scale numbered 1–7 with words describing the hotel at either end. The mid score, 4, indicates that the hotel is neither particularly one nor the other. Please would you tell me the number on the scale which best gives your impression of the hotel.

    (Image) Expensive/inexpensive
                Modern/old-fashioned
                Efficient/inefficient
                Well-known/unknown
                High class/middle class

☐ 15
☐ 16
☐ 17
☐ 18
☐ 19

Q7 Now I would like to discuss the facilities which the hotel offers its guests during their stay.
Would you list for me the various products, facilities and services which this hotel offers its guests?

(1) Bars
(2) Restaurants
(3) Leisure facilities
(4) Functions
(5) Room services (valet, etc.)
(6) Room facilities (TV, etc.)
(7) Reception services
(8) Commercial services (telex, etc.)
(9) Other

If 'other' please state: ....
....
....

(1) ☐	20
(2) ☐	21
(3) ☐	22
(4) ☐	23
(5) ☐	24
(6) ☐	25
(7) ☐	26
(8) ☐	27
(9) ☐	28
☐	29

Q8 (a) Roughly how much time do you spend in the hotel? A lot, some or very little?
(b) Is that mostly in the daytime or evening?

☐ 30

b＼a	A lot	Some	Very little
Daytime	(1)	(2)	(3)
Evening	(4)	(5)	(6)
Both	(7)	(8)	(9)

Q9 While you are staying here your room must cater for many different needs, unlike any single room at home. Do you feel that your room caters for these needs:

(1) Very well
(2) Adequately
(3) Not well enough

☐ 31

Q10 Not counting breakfast, how many of your meals do you expect to take in the hotel during your stay?

(1) Most (all)
(2) Some
(3) Very few (none)

☐ 32

Q11 If you were in the hotel in the evening and wanted a drink, would you:

(1) Have it in your room
(2) Use the hotel bar
(3) Try to find somewhere away from the hotel
(4) Other

☐ 33

If 'other' please state: ....

....

Q12 Now I've asked you about your room, the restaurants and bars, can you recall which products, services and facilities you have actually used during your stay?

–	(6) Room facilities (TV, etc.)	(3) ☐ 34
–	(7) Reception services	(4) ☐ 35
(3) Leisure facilities	(8) Commercial services	(5) ☐ 36
(4) Functions	(9) Other	(6) ☐ 37

(3) Leisure facilities (8) Commercial services
(4) Functions   (9) Other

If 'other' please state: ....

....

(3) ☐ 34
(4) ☐ 35
(5) ☐ 36
(6) ☐ 37
(7) ☐ 38
(8) ☐ 39
(9) ☐ 40

Q13 Can you recall anything at all about the hotel which has displeased you during your stay?

(Record answer) ....

....

....

▨ 41

Q14 Can you recall anything which has particularly pleased you about the hotel during your stay?

(Record answer) ....

....

....

▨ 42

Q15 If the manager here were given a free hand to improve or add to the hotel's products, facilities or services in some way, what changes would *you* like to see in the hotel?

(Record answer) ....

....

....

....

▨ 43

Q16 By the way, have you met the general manager of the hotel?

(1) Yes   (2) No   ☐ 44

Q17 Do you know his name?

(1) Yes   (2) No   ☐ 45

Q18 Now we've talked about different aspects of the hotel, could you give me your impressions about the atmosphere of the place as a whole. Here are half a dozen cards (GIVE CARDS) like the ones I showed you before, with scales numbered 1–7. Would you tell me the number on each scale which best represents your feelings about the hotel's general atmosphere.

     ☐ 46
     ☐ 47
     ☐ 48
     ☐ 49
     ☐ 50

(Atmosphere) Light and airy/dull and gloomy
                 Busy/inactive
                 Noisy/quiet
                 Formal/informal
                 Friendly/unfriendly

Finally, could I ask you a few questions about yourself?

Q19 Are you staying here:
(1) on business
(2) for a holiday
(3) to break your journey   ☐ 51

Q20 Are you staying:
(1) Alone
(2) With one other person
(3) With a group of people   ☐ 52

Q21 Roughly how long will your stay in this hotel be:
(1) 1–2 days
(2) 3–6 days
(3) 1–2 weeks
(4) More than 2 weeks   ☐ 53

Q22 Are you married or single?
(1) Married   (2) Single (widowed, etc.)   ☐ 54

Thank you very much for your help, it has been most interesting talking to you.

Q23 (DO NOT ASK)

AGE

	Up to 35	36 to 65	Over 65
Male	(1)	(2)	(3)
Female	(4)	(5)	(6)

☐ 55

Q24 (DO NOT ASK)

NATIONALITY

(1) British   (2) Overseas

☐ 56

HOTEL CODES

MANCHESTER – Box one

(1)	(5)
(2)	(6)
(3)	(7)
(4)	(8)

OTHERS – Box two

(1)	(4)
(2)	(5)
(3)	(6)

DATE: /   /

Oxfam shoppers' survey

(1)   How long have you lived in your present home?   1 ☐

    1. Under 1 year   ☐

    2. 1–5 years   ☐

    3. 6–10 years   ☐

    4. Over 10 years   ☐

(2)   How often do you go to the Knutsford shopping centre?   ☐

    1. Daily   ☐

    2. 2 or 3 times a week   ☐

    3. Once a week   ☐

    4. 2 or 3 times a month   ☐

    5. Hardly ever   ☐

(3)   What is your usual reason for going there?   ☐

    1. Passing through   ☐

    2. Looking at shops   ☐

    3. Meeting people or having a meal   ☐

    4. Shopping for groceries   ☐

    5. Shopping for other goods   ☐

    6. To work   ☐

(4)   Nowadays people have many calls on their money.
How do you feel about charities asking for help?   ☐

Agree strongly	Agree	No strong feelings	Disagree	Disagree strongly

Appendix B

(5) If you had any money to spare which one, if any, of these
charities would you be prepared to support?

Christian Aid ☐   ☐

Help the Aged ☐

Oxfam ☐

Save the Children ☐

Sue Ryder Society ☐

Another charity ☐ please give name

None ☐

(6) Charities raise money in all the following ways.
Which way do you think raises the most?   ☐

Jumble sales ☐

Street collections ☐

Appeals ☐

Collecting boxes ☐

Shops ☐

(7) Many charities advertise to raise money.
What are your feelings about this method?   ☐

Agree strongly	Agree	No strong feelings	Disagree	Disagree strongly

(8) Could you tell us why you feel this way?
(about question 7)   ☐

_____

_____

_____

162

Appendix B

(9) In some towns there are shops run by charitable organizations. Could you tell us the name of any you know in Knutsford?

_____

_____

☐

(10) Do you know of the Oxfam shop there?

    1. ☐ Yes

    2. ☐ No

If your answer is 'yes' please go to question 11
If your answer is 'no' please go to question 17 and do not answer questions 11–16

(11) Can you remember how you found out about the Oxfam shop?

☐

1. No – can't remember ☐

2. Word of mouth (someone told you) ☐

3. Passing by the shop ☐

4. From newspapers ☐

5. From the radio ☐

6. From television ☐

7. From magazines ☐

(12) Have you ever been into the Oxfam shop there?

☐

    1. ☐ Yes

    2. ☐ No

If your answer is 'yes', continue with question 13
If your answer is 'no', please go on to question 17, and ignore questions 13–16

Appendix B

(13) When was the last time you were in the Oxfam shop in Knutsford?

1. Less than 1 week ago ☐
2. Less than 1 month ☐
3. More than 1 month ☐
4. More than 6 months ago ☐

☐

(14) Have you ever bought anything from the Oxfam shop?

If you *have*, was it:

Second-hand clothes ☐

Other second-hand goods ☐

New craft goods ☐

Other new goods
(stationery) ☐

☐
☐
☐
☐

If you *have not*, please go on to question 17 and leave out questions 15–16

(15) How satisfied were you with your purchase?

☐

Very satisfied	Satisfied	No strong feelings	Dissatisfied	Very dissatisfied

(16) Is there any particular reason why you felt as you do? (please write it down)

☐

_____

_____

_____

164

Appendix B

(17) Do you think Oxfam should set their prices as high as possible, or as low as possible, or neither?

☐

1. High ☐
2. Neither ☐
3. Low ☐

(18) What sort of things do you think Oxfam should sell to raise money?

☐

1. Second-hand clothes ☐ ☐
2. Other second-hand goods ☐ ☐
3. New craft goods? ☐ ☐
4. New stationery ☐ ☐
5. Everything saleable ☐ ☐
6. No opinion ☐ ☐

(19) What is your general impression of Oxfam shops?

Neither

Easy to find	☐	☐	☐	☐	☐ Hard to find	☐
Roomy	☐	☐	☐	☐	☐ Cramped	☐
Expensive	☐	☐	☐	☐	☐ Cheap	☐
Clean	☐	☐	☐	☐	☐ Dirty	☐
Untidy	☐	☐	☐	☐	☐ Tidy	☐
Friendly	☐	☐	☐	☐	☐ Unfriendly	☐

Neither

(20) Do you think Oxfam should spend money on making their shops attractive?

─YES──yes── No strong feeling ──no──NO─→
☐──☐── ☐ ──☐──☐

Appendix B

(21) Where and how do you think the money from Oxfam is spent?

	A lot	Some	A little	None	
Overseas disaster relief	☐	☐	☐	☐	☐
Overseas projects (helping people to help themselves)	☐	☐	☐	☐	☐
Charity in Britain	☐	☐	☐	☐	☐
Administration costs	☐	☐	☐	☐	☐

(22) Where and how do you think the money from Oxfam *should* be spent?

	A lot	Some	A little	None	
Overseas disaster relief	☐	☐	☐	☐	☐
Overseas projects (helping people to help themselves)	☐	☐	☐	☐	☐
Charity in Britain	☐	☐	☐	☐	☐
Administration costs	☐	☐	☐	☐	☐

(23) Personal information (there is no need to write down your name)

SEX   1. Male   ☐   ☐
       2. Female   ☐

(24)

AGE   1. 16–24   ☐   ☐
       2. 25–34   ☐
       3. 35–49   ☐
       4. 50–65   ☐
       5. Over 65   ☐

Appendix B

(25)

    Marital status

    1. Single ☐

    2. Married ☐

    3. Widowed ☐

    4. Divorced ☐

☐

(26)   Have you any children under 16 living with you?

    1. YES ☐

    2. NO ☐

☐

(27)   What is your, or your husband's or wife's job?

_____

_____

This questionnaire will be collected the same day that it was given to you

THANK YOU VERY MUCH FOR YOUR HELP

☐

Appendix C: Recommended reading

Marketing Research
Peter M. Chisnall
McGraw-Hill, 3rd edition, 1986
Comprehensive text widely used in university and polytechnic business degree programmes.

Dictionary of Market Research
P. A. Talmage
The Market Research Society
and
The Incorporated Society of British Advertisers, 1988
Very useful text covering virtually every aspect of market research techniques and applications.

The Marketing Pocket Book
The Advertising Association
Yearly publication of useful reference material covering economic and demographic data, media analyses, advertising expenditures, etc.

Glossary of Marketing Research
European Society for Opinion and Marketing Research (ESOMAR), 1989
Comprehensive listing of 383 market research technical terms in English, French, German, Italian, Spanish and Dutch.

The Industrial Market Research Handbook
Paul N. Hague
Kogan Page, 1988
Practical guide to industrial market research by highly experienced individual marketing specialist.

Consumer Market Research Handbook
(ed.) Robert M. Worcester
McGraw-Hill, 3rd edition, 1989
Collection of articles on consumer market research techniques and uses by leading experts.

Statistics for Marketing
Leslie Rodger
McGraw-Hill, 1984
Comprehensive guide to maths and statistics techniques and their applications in marketing.

Marketing: A Behavioural Analysis
Peter M. Chisnall
McGraw-Hill, 2nd edition, 1985
Comprehensive treatment of the many behavioural factors that influence buying behaviour. Useful guide to development of market and social research designs.

Question Design and Attitude Measurement
A. N. Oppenheim
Heinemann, 1968
Clearly written guide to the basic skills of questionnaire construction.

Survey Methods in Social Investigation
C. A. Moser and G. Kalton
Heinemann, 1971
Classic text on survey methodology.

Strategic Industrial Marketing
Peter M. Chisnall
Prentice Hall, 2nd edition, 1989
Strategic approach to marketing of goods and services in industrial, technical, commercial and non-profit (public sector/charity) organizations. Includes section on industrial marketing research.

Survey Research for Managers
Peter F. Hutton
Macmillan, 1988
Pragmatic guide amplified by case studies illustrating how decision makers have benefited from applying market research to a wide range of business problems.

Useful Data for Market Researchers
Market Research Society, 1990
Highly relevant 'background' data for market research purposes; up to date and well-presented sets of key data.

Appendix D:
Case histories

CASE 1: *The Mystery of Declining Sales*   Sue Williams
(How a project for Agatha Christie books resulted in increased sales)

CASE 2: *The Market for Crisps*   Robert Fairweather
(The case of a brand with its roots firmly in the regions)

CASE 3: *The Public Good*   Richard Windle
(The use of survey research by local government for assessing the opinions and needs of consumers)

CASE 4: *Taking the Low Road*   Barry Lee
(The research programme that culminated in the launch of Courage's new low alcohol lager, Carlton LA)

CASE 5: *Ethnic Minorities*   Paul Gildon
(An examination of some of the problems of researching ethnic minorities)

CASE 6: *Earthmovers*   Geoffrey Faulder
(A market entry study for the Hertz Corporation)

CASE 7: *Evaluating Direct Selling Effectiveness*
(Research aimed to discover why agents selling direct to homes varied considerably in their selling performance)

CASE 8: *Evaluating Sports Sponsorship*   David Smith
(A major chemical and plastics company commissioned a market research agency to evaluate the effectiveness of sponsorship of a ladies' tennis tournament)
    As a result of the research findings, the company decided to extend sponsorship and to devise a new strategy to ensure that they benefited fully from the support given to these events.

171

Case 1: The mystery of declining sales

In March 1985 William Collins, the publishers, held the largest franchise from Agatha Christie's estate to market her books. Unfortunately, sales were declining and Collins were uncertain whether this reflected declining interest in crime as a category, whether this author had had her day, or whether some other factor (like, for example, declining interest in reading and buying paperback books) was responsible.

James R. Adams and Associates were asked to put forward proposals for research to identify the problem and provide some indications for rectifying this situation. Publishing companies are not renowned for commissioning and conducting market research. In fact, Collins were new to market research themselves. For them, the step towards research was extremely innovative, setting them apart from other companies in this area of business. The resultant success of this move and the extreme vigour employed by the company in putting our recommendations into action highlights their innovative approach to business.

This paper deals with the investigation; it shows how market research can help solve even the most 'sinister' of problems and highlights how, when implemented correctly, it can be of great financial benefit to the client.

Considering the problem

Our first step was to consider what problems may lie behind the situation. There could have been several reasons for declining sales in Christie paperbacks. We hypothesized that any of the following could have a negative effect on sales:

Reading is in decline, under the influence of TV viewing.

Paperback sales are in decline, due to the economic situation.

Crime fiction is a declining category; horror and science fiction are current favourites.

Agatha Christie is being replaced as a crime writer by newer authors.

Agatha Christie is popular with older readers. As they die off, they are not being replaced by the younger readers.

Presentation of Agatha Christie books (cover designs, point of sale displays, etc.) are not sufficiently competitive.

Effective distribution for these titles is not as good as that of the competition.

Promotional activities may be inadequate.

We recommend a mix of desk research, qualitative and quantitative research to find out whether any of these hypotheses were the cause of declining sales. Our research proposal was necessarily flexible, since information gained from one piece of research could affect action at later stages.

In the event, we discovered a solution to the problem of declining sales relatively early on in the research process and therefore did not have to test every hypothesis originally put forward.

The initial investigation

The first question we needed to answer was whether reading itself was in decline and, following on from that, whether paperback sales were suffering as a result. The best source for answering these questions was Target Group Index (TGI), which had been monitoring paperback buyers since 1978.

These data were purchased and analysed. The analysis showed that the number of adults claiming to have bought a paperback in the previous twelve months had declined from 20.9 million (1978) to 19.6 million (1984). In percentage terms (taking into account any change in population), the decline amounted to about 5 per cent – less than 1 per cent a year. Although this was not good news, it did show that the rate of decline in Agatha Christie sales was not an inevitable consequence of market forces.

TGI also enabled us to work out the profile of paperback buyers and those who had bought more than ten paperbacks a year ('heavy buyers'). We found that the total market was biased towards the young, those in higher socio-economic groups, and better educated. The latter two findings were not surprising, although the bias in socio-economic grade was balanced in absolute terms by the larger numbers of people in the lower groups.

In terms of sex of paperback buyers, men were just as likely to be heavy buyers as women. Geographic spread was fairly even, with about half the population in each television region claiming to be paperback buyers. London accounted for nearly 26 per cent of the market, with the Central television area accounting for 18 per cent.

The real detective work

Having discovered that there had not been a dramatic decline in the numbers of people claiming to buy paperback books, the next task was to find out whether crime fiction was having less appeal and, specifically, whether Christie herself was having less appeal. We also needed to see whether the presentation of Christie had had anything to do with the declining sales.

Unfortunately, TGI provided no information about reading different genres or, specifically, reading different authors. The next stage of research had to answer several questions, some of which were complex and difficult. The route taken was qualitative, through group discussions.

We normally conduct a qualitative stage of research prior to quantification since it is important to know what types of questions to ask and how to ask them. Apart from this, a qualitative route was chosen because we needed in-depth information about people's attitudes to a number of different subjects. We also needed an opportunity to show respondents several different prompts and gain their reactions to these. A qualitative approach would also give us the licence to probe areas which could come up spontaneously in a group situation.

Four groups were held with current readers of Christie (i.e. those claiming to have read an Agatha Christie book within the last two years). In every group, all respondents were buyers of paperback books (i.e. they had to have claimed to have bought a paperback book themselves in the last twelve months).

Groups

The TGI profiles helped to determine the types of people we needed to talk to. Two different ages of respondents were recruited: 15–24 years old and 35–44 years old. It was felt that the 35–44-year-old age group would be able to provide useful additional information on the sub-teen and older ages. Thus, we would be able to find out if this older group was passing books down to other members of the family (like sons and daughters), for example. This we could then check with the 15–24-year-olds.

All groups were mixed in terms of sex and two of the four were ABC1 socio-economic grade spectrum; it was felt that C2Ds ought to be included since they represented an important slice of the market in terms of actual numbers.

In terms of location, two were held in the London area and the remaining two in the Central TV area – the two most important regions, when looking at the profile of paperback buyers.

Discussions in the four groups had to cover a lot of ground. First of all, we needed to find out what place reading had in the respondents' lives and what different types of fiction they read. We also wanted to find out how people went about buying books and what was important to this buying process. We had to discover, in detail, how they viewed crime in relation to other genres. Christie needed to be probed in full, with emphasis on any differences between her style and other writers, if they existed.

Apart from this detailed discussion we also had to make sure that we had enough time to expose the groups to the Christie cover designs. Over the course of twenty years the way in which the author had been presented in terms of cover design had changed radically. The company was able to provide us with examples of each type of design; often books of the same title.

At the end of each group we covered the influence of television and films: whether watching a Christie series or film actually helped or hindered the purchasing of Christie books.

Information gained from readers was interesting and surprising. It also seemed to provide a possible clue to the solution of the problem. However, we felt that a repeat with non-readers would be advisable, to see whether they responded in a similar way to Christie readers. Thus, a further four groups were conducted with these individuals: those who had shown an interest in Christie (by watching Christie films and/or television serials) but had not followed this interest through by reading a Christie book within the last two years. Non-readers also had to have shown an interest in crime fiction by reading at least one of a number of specified crime writers. In terms of demographic profile and paperback buying behaviour, these respondents matched those in the Christie readers' groups.

Topics covered were the same, although emphasis was placed on why these respondents were not buying Christie books, despite showing an interest in Christie by watching television and films.

In the event, both reader and non-reader groups lasted an average of an hour and a half each, some of the groups lasting as long as two hours.

From the qualitative stage we learnt in great depth about the buying of paperback books and the place of reading in respondents' lives. The buying process had, in fact, several distinct stages, each of varying importance. This store of knowledge has since been used repeatedly by the client. Discussions about different types of fiction indicated that there was a great deal of interest in the crime genre.

One possible reason for the decline in sales was the idea that Christie had had her day. However, the qualitative work revealed that Christie was viewed as the 'queen of crime'; the idea that Christie was in any way passée as an author received no support, even from non-readers. Christie had, in fact, several benefits perceived as unique to her which other crime writers were not seen to have. Her writing requires active reading – always trying, and always failing, to guess the identity of the murderer; the murders in her books are always 'nice'; her detailed style invites participation; and you never grow out of her.

The principal difference between the two sets of individuals was that non-readers had stopped reading Christie – hardly any had not read her at some point. Most non-readers could not give cogent reasons for stopping.

Interestingly, we found that media exposure (specifically television and/or films) could have a detrimental effect on reading Christie. Reading a book is a very active pastime, where the reader often imagines the characters in the book and has ideas about their appearance and personality. Listening to radio plays was seen as very similar to reading. Visual presentation can destroy this enjoyment since it is another person's portrayal of a character. Therefore, if the central character of the book is thought to be miscast, this can distort the pleasure the viewer gets.

With Christie, this visual presentation is even more important: the bulk of her books feature either Poirot or Miss Marple. Thus, being put off by the main character does not only put the viewer off that book; it can also put them off any book featuring the same character. This problem was encountered with Poirot; his portrayal was criticized in many groups.

Apart from this, a television presentation of Christie deters the viewer from buying *that* book since the whole point of reading Christie is to guess 'whodunnit'; although it may encourage the viewer to buy others (bearing in mind the point above).

Since Christie as an author did not appear to be the reason for declining sales another possible reason could be the presentation of Christie. Examples of Christie cover designs from the 1960s through to 1984 were presented to respondents. Here we were looking for appropriateness of design as well as likes and dislikes. The groups were consistent in their reactions: the current covers did not convey the qualities of the author; in fact, they were wholly inappropriate. These current covers often featured blood and gore. Here we found our solution to the mystery. The problem had arisen because the book market had changed with the rise in the sales of horror books. Although no explicit policy had been consciously implemented, cover designs for Christie had been influenced by this trend.

The situation was a classic example of the double turn-off. Christie readers turn away from the more gory aspects of crime; there may be a whole series of violent deaths in her books, but there is no dwelling on the details. As mentioned previously, her readers classed her books as having 'nice murders'. Thus, horror-style covers were repelling her natural market. On the other hand, we hypothesized, those who were attracted by these designs and were looking for blood and thunder were very disappointed by what they found.

When the books were first presented respondents were certain that they were horror books, despite being clearly labelled with the Agatha Christie name. What happened was that there was conflict on the covers. Christie said one thing, the picture another. Thus, the cover designs were actually inhibiting sales, not helping them.

From discussions about how respondents buy books we found that the cover design was extremely important. Psychologically it could be the case that, in situations of conflict or mismatch, a pictorial image tends to dominate words; therefore pictures are processed more quickly than words. Or it could be that salience could lead to selective attention of the pictorial information. To date, there has been no published academic work investigating this area, as far as we know.

Putting the solution into action

It was recommended that the problem with the Christie cover designs should be resolved prior to any further investigations. The qualitative research gave strong indications as to how Christie should be presented. Given specific guidelines on these issues, Collins acted with considerable vigour.

Collins produced a very impressive sales pack for their representatives to use when calling on their customers (the booksellers). Included in the pack was information about the qualitative research and some top line results. Sales reps were able to go into bookshops armed with the information and knowledge that, for example, Christie was still viewed as the 'Queen of Crime'. This received a very warm reaction from the trade, who were unused to being party to such information. A sales campaign to the retail trade was also launched, highlighting Christie as 'Queen', with a spend of £25,000.

Totally new packaging was created and we went back to a new set of groups of readers about ten months later, to check that the problems had been overcome. Since non-readers held similar views to readers, it was considered that we need only check the new packaging with readers of Christie.

These four groups of Christie readers were identical in group structure to those which we had previously recruited. Two groups were of the ages 15–24; two aged 35–44. In terms of socio-economic grade, two groups were ABC1 and two were C2D. Two were conducted in the London area and the remaining two in the Central TV area. The groups confirmed the previous work: the 'horror' covers were wholly inappropriate. The new designs carried all the right messages: they were seen as ideal for Christie.

These new designs were seen as intriguing and subtle, which reflected the way the author wrote. They were also not misleading; it could be seen at a glance that they were Christie paperbacks. The pictures on the front of the books were seen to link with the title, which was very important, without giving any of the story away. The covers also gave the impression of quality. Most importantly, the name of the author was presented in large lettering. This new theme for the covers, concentrating on murder, mystery and intrigue, was developed into point of sale and other advertising. This was also tested in the groups and received a warm response.

Since Collins was responsible for sixty-eight Christie titles it was not physically possible to change the cover designs overnight. Instead, six new designs were implemented within four months.

A further stage of research was recommended to quantify these results. However, events overtook us. The response from the trade was so positive and increased orders were coming so fast that Collins could not spare the time to delay changing the other Christie covers.

We had managed to discount many of the hypotheses that we had originally put forward. We knew that the decline in sales was not due to a decline in reading or buying paperback books, from the initial TGI stage of research.

From the qualitative work, we knew that crime fiction was alive and well and that the problem did not lie with Christie herself because she was viewed as the Queen of Crime, even among non-readers. We also knew that her audience was not declining; that she was still popular with young readers.

Problems with distribution of her books were discounted since, in the publishing industry, booksellers can stock books and get full returns if they do not sell them.

In terms of promotion, actual exposure of Christie on television showed a slight decline over the period. In 1982 there had been seventeen hours; in 1983 twelve hours; and in 1984 ten-and-a-quarter hours. (Subsequently, this level was maintained through 1985 and 1986, later increasing to more than twenty hours in 1987.) The presentation of Agatha Christie books was the only other hypothesis left unanswered.

As a result of this combination of activities (cover design changes and presentations to the trade), sales of Agatha Christie paperbacks increased.

Case 2: The market for crisps

If you were asked to name the brand leaders in Great Britain among food products which would you bring to mind? Probably Heinz Tomato Soup, Kellogg's Corn Flakes, Rowntree's Kit-Kat, Bird's Eye Fish Fingers and Pedigree Chum and Whiskas. All these major and long-established brands have wide recognition and would be acknowledged almost universally as market leaders. They are all available throughout Great Britain.

One major brand that might not come to mind quite as quickly – but which is now of equal stature – is Walker's Crisps. Yet this market leader is not even generally on sale in Scotland or in North East or South West England and the main reason why it would probably not be named is that its roots are firmly in the regions. Indeed, it has been advertised on television in London only since 1985.

The first advertising for the brand in London led to a complaint to the Advertising Standards Authority. It was a poster and tube-card campaign showing packets of crisps coming along a country road under the headline 'Welcome to Britain's best-selling crisps'. The complainant argued that this was a false claim, but the complaint was rejected. Walker's *was* already Britain's best-selling crisp before being launched in London.

When we showed the poster in research groups in London it evoked shock and disbelief. Londoners could not believe that any brand with which they were unfamiliar could possibly be a market leader. Five years later our research indicates that Walker's is the best-rated of any crisp brand in London and many other areas where it is available. It is interesting to discover how the brand has achieved this in such a short time and in a very competitive market.

The story started in Leicester in 1948. Walker's was a small chain of pork butchers. Meat supplies were severely restricted because of post-war shortages, the shops were sold out by 10.00 a.m. each day and the factory was working at half capacity. The company wanted to find a way to use the work-force and also to overcome the summer lull in the sale of pork products. They considered diversifying into ice cream production but became concerned that bacteriological problems could arise if meat and dairy products were manufactured together. They then opted for potato crisps.

Production began in 1949. The potatoes were cut by hand on a vegetable slicer and the crisps cooked in a fish and chip shop frier. Salt was sprinkled by hand to make the crisps ready salted. The crisps quickly became popular locally and new production premises were opened in 1951. Sales continued to grow rapidly, especially after a new automatic cooker was bought from America and installed in 1959. It was one of the first in Europe and it gave a great boost to production capacity. Within a further ten years Walker's had become the dominant crisp brand inn the Midlands while Golden Wonder and Smiths together controlled some 70 per cent of the crisp market nationally.

In 1967 Walker's recognized the need to engage in marketing as well as selling, so they recruited John Cullip from Golden Wonder, which was based just a few miles away in Market Harborough, as Sales and Marketing Manager. More than twenty years later this role has broadened and he is now the Commercial Director. When John Cullip joined the company it had substantial excess production capacity. Within three years that was no longer the case and for most of the time since then demand for Walker's Crisps has outstripped supply. One of his first moves was to increase the number of packs in a Walker's carton from thirty-six to forty-eight. Customers continued to order the same number of cartons, so there was an immediate 30% turnover increase.

The late 1960s saw the growth of multiple food retailers. The conventional wisdom at that time was that for a brand to be successful it had to be stocked in supermarkets. Yet Walker's did not supply these outlets – partly because it was felt that they would try to enforce terms that were unattractive but also to avoid increased distribution costs. Instead, the customer franchise was developed by means of heavy telephone advertising and distribution went through the wholesale trade to independent outlets and pubs.

Short lines of distribution helped to ensure product freshness and this reinforced consumer belief in the product's superiority. Even today in most parts of the country anybody buying and eating a packet of Walker's Crisps is probably consuming a product that was manufactured just a few days before.

From the beginning of his time with Walker's, John Cullip has believed in maintaining both the strength of the brand's consumer franchise and its profitability. The two have developed together. As early as 1970 this regional brand was more profitable than its two big competitors together with their then far greater market share.

In 1973 the brand was extended into Yorkshire and Anglia – still selling to the consumer primarily through independent shops and pubs. In these areas supermarket sales of crisps suffered as consumers bought Walker's rather than the crisps they stocked. The key to the brand's success has been Walker's consistent investment in its product quality; advertising has fuelled demand and has led consumers to ask for Walker's Crisps. This, in turn, has forced often unwilling outlets to stock the brand.

Data from a trade survey using thirty-two individual depth and sixty-four semi-structured interviews with forty-eight publicans, twenty-four grocers and twenty-four proprietors of CTNs indicated that many independent retailers resented having to stock Walker's. They expressed the view that other brands available from wholesalers or cash and carries were much cheaper and offered greater scope for profit. From time to time they were tempted by a particularly attractive special offer, but their sales fell as consumers went elsewhere in search of Walker's.

Since John Cullip joined Walker's there has been consistent heavy investment in television advertising. It is the marketing equivalent of the vicious circle. Make a good product, ensure people know about it and keep telling them.

In the late 1970s the supermarket chain share of sale for most food products rose quickly and seemingly inexorably, yet Walker's Crisps continued to sell through independents. Gradually the hard-nosed buyers in these chains realized that the growth of their share of the crisp market was hampered because they did not stock the brand their customers wanted. Eventually Asda opened a branch in Leicester and decided that they could not afford to be without Walker's Crisps. In 1980 they started selling Walker's – at a premium to other brands. Despite the higher price, Walker's outsold their competitors.

In 1982 a tiny article at the back of the *Observer* magazine featured a crisp-tasting in which Walker's was rated the best brand. The next morning the Sainsbury buyer was on the phone to Walker's sales manager. Sainsbury wanted to stock this 'best brand'. Soon they started to do so – but at first only in a few outlets. Today Walker's Crisps sell very well through most Sainsbury branches.

Attitude Research Ltd began working for Walker's in 1975. Apart from crisps Walker's also sold savoury snacks. One brand – Snaps – was aimed at children and their mothers and was marketed as a low-price children's snack. Our first project was to look at Snaps and see how sales could be improved. We found that mothers and young children were not aware that the product sold for 3p, whereas crisps cost 5p. When they learnt of the price difference they became very enthusiastic. We reported accordingly and the price was then featured prominently on-pack and in new television advertising. Sales leapt. After that we were called in from time to time to obtain consumer reaction to a variety of aspects of the marketing mix for both crisps and savoury snacks.

Walker's found that often they wanted to know about consumer attitudes to a particular topic but that the issue did not justify a complete research study. They decided that they wanted a regular look at all aspects of the market through consumer eyes and in 1979 Attitude Research began Market Track (MT). Twice a year we conduct a series of group discussions in which we ask consumers to give us their views on the potato crisp and shaped crisp market – products, flavours, brands, packs, advertising, etc. This is then followed once a year by a major quantitative survey in which we interview 1,080 people who buy and/or eat relevant products. This tracking has enabled Walker's to plan their marketing activity with comprehensive and always up to date understanding of consumer attitudes.

In working for Walker's we have throughout presented our findings to the same Marketing Team. John Cullip still attends these presentations. The Marketing Manager is now Richard Gregory, who joined Walker's in 1972 as a Product Manager. This continuity has ensured that nobody wastes time and effort trying to reinvent the wheel and that briefing meetings do not need to repeat each time a description of the market.

One of Walker's strengths lies in the continuity of its relationship with its suppliers. Walker's is not averse to working with relatively small (and often local) companies. The advertising agency for crisps – Meares, Langley, Moore – is based in Leicester and has held the account since 1974. Communication Research Ltd has regularly conducted quantitative advertising tests since 1980. Since 1984 the Oxford Market Research Agency has conducted regular quantitative product tests to help Walker's to ensure that their crisps are developed in line with changing consumer tastes. During the course of our tracking studies in the early 1980s we found that housewives were increasingly keen to buy multipacks of crisps but just as Walker's went into supermarkets in their own time, they did so too, with multipacks. For Walker's the problem was that consumers had become accustomed to paying less for bulk packs while the manufacturing cost of the extra packaging operation added to production costs. Companies producing multipacks were packing them – expensively – by hand.

After extensive trials and assistance with technical development Walker's were eventually satisfied that they had a machine that successfully packed multipacks automatically to their high standards. Only then did they start to market them. The strength of the brand was by then so great that unlike its competitors Walker's did not have to sell crisps in multipacks for a lower price than standard packs. In our most recent Market Track survey we have found that the Walker's multipacks have made a major contribution to the brand's continuing growth.

At a time when supermarket brands are taking an increasing share of many food markets, the sales and market share of Walker's Crisps are still increasing. The brand is still not national yet it is a market leader. Walker's current market share for crisps – 33 per cent (sterling) – is now more than twice that of any other manufacturer's brand. Its high reputation among consumers is still developing. In our research, when asked to name the best brand of crisps, far more customers named Walker's than any other brand. Furthermore the number is increasing rapidly.

This Leicester-based company has remained true to its roots. In the 1990s it is likely to become much more widely recognized for the strength of the Walker's brand and the sales and marketing success that have been achieved.

Case 3: The public good

Local government in Britain is responsible for spending of more than £40 billion and, as such, is one of the main suppliers of goods and services in the country. Today the role and responsibilities of Local Authorities are being examined more closely than at any time since the end of the last century. Far-reaching changes are planned in the fields of education, housing and finance while a wide range of services that have traditionally been provided by local government are soon to be put out to competitive tender. The argument about whether these changes are desirable or not has focused attention on the quality of services that are provided. Certainly quality needs to be taken into account and, as with other things, the cheapest may not necessarily be the best value for money.

Survey research can be useful when it comes to measuring how efficiently services are provided, since much of the information that is routinely collected for this purpose is based on existing users of services. In this context the efficiency of the library service might be measured by the number of books issued while the equivalent measure within the housing department would be the number of repairs carried out. While both of these statistics are useful they do not tell the whole story. The number of book issues and the size of the stock need to be set against whether people find the books they are interested in and whether the library provides the information they need. The number of housing repairs needs to be taken in conjunction with how satisfied customers are with the standard of workmanship. The best way to find the answers to these questions is to ask people what they think.

In planning services Local Authorities have an obligation to ensure that they are identifying the needs of the community, that these needs are being met effectively and that resources are allocated as fairly as possible between different groups. To achieve this, information is available from a number of sources. Demand can be measured by the number of users of a service, the number of admissions to a sports centre, for example, or the number of enquiries received about a particular activity. Satisfaction can be gauged by the number of complaints. The need for new services or alterations to existing arrangements can be brought to the Authority's notice by pressure groups or interested individuals. In addition there is constant feedback through the elected representatives and from Council employees.

Each of these components has a part to play in a system that is democratically accountable. It can be argued, however, that there is a need to go further to find out the views of non-users or those whose interests are not represented by pressure groups. This is where survey research, which can be seen as a means of consulting all residents on an equal basis, is a useful tool.

In the commercial world, research is used extensively. By consulting consumers, products can be fine-tuned to match what people want and potentially disastrous new product launches can be avoided. The same concept can be applied to service provision by local authorities. Although profit is not the motivation, authorities do have a duty to ensure that their resources are used as effectively as possible. Surveys can be carried out among specific groups within the population to investigate particular problems or, as is increasingly the case, more general surveys can be used to ascertain the views of residents across a wide range of services. The type of information that can be provided by this sort of study can be looked at in three ways.

First, the potential demand for services can be ascertained. This may well be greater than is indicated by the number of existing users. Some people may not be aware that a particular service is available or the way in which it is delivered may be inconvenient. Where major investment decisions are required the need for consultation is even greater. A survey might be used, for example, to gauge whether there is sufficient demand for the construction of a new leisure facility and, if so, where it might best be located. This could be done before large sums of money are committed.

Secondly, satisfaction with existing services can be measured. Relying on the number of complaints can be misleading and does tend to over-emphasize negative aspects. If people are full of praise for the courtesy and efficiency of the refuse collection team it is unlikely that they will write to the Council and say so, but this information is useful if changes to the service are proposed. On the other hand, if there are genuine problems these can be quantified far more effectively by a survey of opinion than by an analysis of letters of complaint.

Finally, and perhaps most importantly, the effectiveness of communication between the Council and the community can be examined. At a general level it is useful for an Authority to know whether people are aware of what it is doing and whether its overall image is favourable. If there are problems in this direction these may be overcome by a local publicity campaign or the production of community newsletters. At a more specific level an Authority needs to know how people find out what is going on locally and this will indicate how it can make them aware of the services that are on offer.

As well as giving their reactions to existing services consumers can also be asked to choose between different options for future priorities. In this way they can be actively involved in the decision making process.

One Authority that has consulted its electors in this way is Strathkelvin District Council, one of nineteen Districts in the Strathclyde region of Scotland. Strathkelvin covers an area of some sixty-four square miles stretching from the outskirts of Glasgow in the south to the Campsie Fells in the north. It comprises two main towns, Kirkintilloch and Bishopbriggs. The District was created in 1975 by combining the two town councils with adjacent rural areas. As often happens with reorganizations in local government it can be difficult for people to identify with the area covered by the new Authority.

Conscious of this the District Council has, over the past few years, been working hard to establish an identity. A new logo has been introduced along with the slogan 'Changing for the Better' to describe the changes that have been taking place. A survey of local residents was commissioned as part of this strategy to investigate how much people were aware of what the Council was doing and what they saw as being the main problems that it should be tackling. Initiatives had also been undertaken to help local businesses in the area and part of the research was geared towards finding out what local businessmen saw as the priorities.

Personal interviews were carried out with a representative sample of residents spread across the District and telephone interviews with local businessmen. It was evident from the research that there was a lot of goodwill towards the Council, particularly among older members of the community. The general perception was that they were doing the best they could with the money available. People were not aware, however, of some of the changes the Council had introduced, particularly in the Housing Department, suggesting that it may take time for these to filter through. Satisfaction with services provided by the Council was high, although some problems were identified.

A constant theme in the answers given to questions about the area was that there should be more provision for young people and there was a lot of support for the idea of building a new sports centre. There was also considerable disquiet in some parts of the district that the Council had withdrawn the dog warden service and its reintroduction was seen as a priority by those in the areas most affected. Among the business community there was reasonable optimism for the future and support for the Council's initiatives. Overall the survey produced much detailed information about the views of the community which can be built into the planning process. With limited resources it will not be possible to satisfy all the demands, but at least residents have been consulted as a basis for establishment priorities.

In more general terms it is evident that, while survey research can provide a useful input, it is not a panacea and cannot, in itself, determine priorities. Any action that is taken will need to be decided by politicians or Council officers.

While a survey may indicate that some services are failing to meet the needs of particular groups in the community, it is up to the policy makers to decide whether the situation should be remedied and what level of resource can be allocated to achieve this. Used properly the survey method can be seen as an important part of the democratic process and a means by which electors can be consulted on the specifics of policy once they have indicated their general preferences via the ballot-box.

Case 4: Taking the low road

Low alcohol beers are very much a part of today's drinking scene, but their acceptance as products with the credibility to stand their ground alongside their alcoholic equivalents in pubs and clubs is a remarkably recent phenomenon. When, in the summer of 1987, Courage commissioned Public Attitude Surveys (PAS) to test consumers' reactions to two different brands of low alcohol lager, PAS data from its continuous Drinks Market survey showed that only 1 per cent of adults were drinking any non- or low alcohol beers ('NAB/LABs' as they came to be known) in pubs and clubs in an average week. In the space of twelve months, this penetration was to shoot up to 2.4 per cent – clearly this was an important new market, in which it was vital not only to establish brands but, through market research, to understand the consumer's viewpoint and hence get the brand positioning right.

Extensive qualitative research undertaken by BMP Davidson Pearce suggested that the market growth was happening almost *in spite of* the positioning of existing brands. An increasingly confident consumer did not need to be patronized by claims that low/no alcohol lager 'tastes like real lager', nor to be given rational justifications such as avoiding drinking and driving. The time was right to stop trading on a defensive platform and create a brand that offered itself as a positive choice.

At the time of the PAS research, Courage pubs had been stocking Swan Special Light low alcohol lager for some time. However, when Courage became part of the Elders Brewing Group new brand options were opened up; in addition to the full strength Foster's brand, Elders' Carlton & United Brewery in Australia had a successful low alcohol lager in the form of Carlton Special Light. The research question that Courage posed to PAS was 'would Carlton be at least as acceptable as Swan Light to the British drinker or, indeed, preferred to it?

The approach adopted by PAS, at a number of hall locations, was 'paired comparison', in which lager drinkers tried Carlton and Swan, first 'blind' (with no indication of what brands they were drinking), and then 'branded' (in which the drinker was made aware of the branding by serving himself from a can). Given the rapid expansion of the market, it was important to gauge the reactions of *potential* low alcohol lager drinkers, rather than just those who had already tried it. Those recruited to the product test, therefore, comprised current drinkers of canned lager who thought it likely that they would drink any low alcohol lager in the coming six months.

The results of the 'blind' testing showed that, when the two products were compared without the aid of branding and pack design, Carlton was preferred by as many trialists as was Swan – in fact, slightly more chose Carlton (51 per cent against 48 per cent), but not enough for the difference to be statistically significant. When the test was repeated *branded* (pouring the lager from the can), Carlton was preferred by 52 per cent against Swan's 44 per cent – a difference significant at the 95 per cent level.

Further analysis of the PAS results gave Courage valuable diagnostic indicators about both the product and the branding/surface design. Major product advantages emerged for Carlton: more than two-thirds of trialists thought it 'about right' for colour, while over 80 per cent described Swan as 'too pale'; six in ten said Carlton's head size was right, but over half felt Swan had 'not enough head'; two-thirds chose to say that Swan had 'not enough body', compared with only 39 per cent saying this of Carlton.

The PAS findings gave Courage the 'green light' to introduce the Australian-brewed Carlton Special Light into its pubs in place of Swan Light, and this was done. It was also clear, however, in this rapidly expanding market, that further product and brand development was required to support the next major move – a £2.6 million investment in Courage's Berkshire brewery to brew low alcohol lager in the UK. The next stage in the research programme was to measure the standing of Carlton Special Light against not only Swan but other low alcohol lagers already established in the market place.

Courage, therefore, commissioned a multi-product sensory test, this time from Martin Hamblin Research. Sensory testing aims to provide improved techniques for measuring consumer preferences and requirements in a wide range of product fields. A key factor in the sensitivity of this method is the application of 'magnitude estimation scaling', which makes use of numbers developed by consumers themselves rather than a predetermined verbal scale. Respondents are not pre-selected according to their sensory acuity or numerical adroitness – everybody can easily cope with the scaling method – and, in international research, the problem of producing comparable verbal scales in different languages is avoided. The low alcohol brands tested in addition to Carlton and Swan were Clausthaler, Dansk LA and

Tennents LA. Also included was Kaliber, which belongs to the category of *non*-alcoholic lagers (i.e. completely alcohol free). Trialists at the 'blind' stage were simply told that they were trying different 'lagers', with no reference to their alcohol content. At this stage, the results showed no significant differences between the overall rating of any of the products, although the indications were of a preference for low alcohol, rather than non-alcoholic, lager.

When the lagers were tried branded, all the scores went down. This is unusual, in that once brand values are introduced a product's rating is normally enhanced. It was surmised that this response reflected the relatively poor opinion of low alcohol lagers *per se* at that time (July 1988).

On the basis of this test, the performance of Carlton Special Light was judged by Martin Hamblin as middling to good. Confirming the earlier PAS findings, the product's colour and head were rated particularly favourably – a crucial point, since the old adage that people 'drink with their eyes' has been repeatedly demonstrated in drinks research. While not spectacular, this performance was felt by Courage to justify further development work.

Reaching a packaging solution for a brand that was to be positioned as a positive, confident choice in its own right needed care. In essence, Courage wanted packaging that was a 'badge'. Rather than hide the fact that he was drinking LA, the consumer could be bold and proud of his choice. In the public arena of the pub, a can of Carlton LA should make as much of a statement as drinking from a bottle of Grolsch.

The next stage of product testing took place seven months later, when trial production had started in the UK, a new name 'Carlton LA' had been adopted and a new can design developed. In a further sensory test, newly formulated Carlton LA was compared blind and branded with what were perceived as its three main competitors, Tennents LA, Swan Special Light and the non-alcoholic Kaliber. Also tested, blind only, was the original Australian-brewed product, Carlton Special Light.

The 'overall liking' results from this test are shown in Figure D.1. The most pleasing aspect for Courage was the fact that, in the blind test, Carlton LA was the most liked low alcohol lager – although again, most of the differences were not statistically significant. However, Carlton LA was significantly preferred to Kaliber, the NAB/LAB brand leader at that stage. Furthermore, Carlton LA's branded performance was also seen as encouraging, given that it was a relatively little known brand name facing the firmly established and heavily advertised names of Tennents and Kaliber.

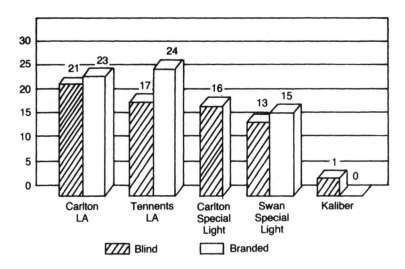

Figure D.1 How the brands rated for overall liking

More general evidence from this test suggested major attitudinal changes since the previous sensory test, only seven months earlier. Positive responses overall were more numerous than before, and the branded scores for the low alcohol products were now *higher* than the blind scores – evidence of the rapid improvement in the credibility of this burgeoning product field. According to Stats MR, this period has seen a major shift in the focus of sales growth from non-alcoholic to low alcohol brands. The non-alcoholic share of total NAB/LAB sales fell from 58 per cent in December 87/January 88 to only 27 per cent in December 88/January 89 – further endorsing Courage's decision to 'take the low road'.

Thus, everything pointed to Courage having an excellent product, both in terms of taste delivery and branding. An integrated programme of market research had enabled the Courage Marketing Department to make major decisions with confidence, leading to the launch of canned Carlton LA in March 1989, with a draught version scheduled for launch this summer.

Case 5: Ethnic minorities

Ethnic minorities are now an important part of any market, but researching them presents particular problems.

All market research is about gathering data from individuals – facts, opinions, attitudes, but there are many different ways of obtaining these data and many different levels of 'truth'. For example, there is a world of difference between the 'hard' truth of 'I live in a terraced house' from the 'soft' or hypothetical truth of 'If I won the pools I would buy a yacht.' Equally, there are some questions (for example, 'What is happening to my market share?') where a precise numerical measure is, if not essential, certainly highly desirable. For other questions (for example, 'What do consumers like about my commercial?') a verbal, descriptive answer is more useful and money spent on obtaining precise figures could well be considered wasted.

The kind of questions to be asked, and the use to which the answers will be put, will often determine the choice between quantitative and qualitative research. Very briefly, the key differences between these approaches can be summarized as follows:

Quantitative research

Large samples, statistically representative of the population, allowing detailed analysis of results; structured questions, which can be administered identically and unambiguously by many different interviewers; clearly defined questions; large number of interviewers; essentially enumerative.

Qualitative research

Small samples, big enough to avoid major errors, but not always sufficient to allow a detailed breakdown of results; relatively unstructured, open-ended questions: they can be modified, refined, added to, as the research proceeds; often loosely defined questions; small number of interviewers; essentially descriptive.

Qualitative techniques are often used in exploratory research where the actual questions to be asked are not fully determined, or the consumer language not yet understood. This can pave the way for a more defined follow-up quantitative stage.

Research with ethnic minorities tends to be exploratory because there is so little precedent for it. Where there are no existing data a descriptive answer to questions (for example, 'How do Indian housewives in the UK use milk?') is often adequate as a starting-point. In ethnic minority research the scope and limits for interviewing may be only partially understood (for example, how closely can an interviewer question a Muslim housewife on dietary laws?).

All these factors mean that, in the ethnic minority research I have conducted, qualitative research has predominated. Its techniques are mainly group discussions and depth interviews, usually conducted by interviewers matched ethnically to respondents. In a group discussion eight similar people – for example, young working class second generation West Indians – will be brought together in a relaxed social atmosphere. The group moderator is trained to stimulate the group to talk within certain guidelines without directing them or influencing them with his own opinions. By conducting several such groups and examining the tape recordings or transcripts of them he can build up a clear descriptive account of 'qualitative' questions – for example, how do young West Indians compare the key brands of very strong lagers, or what are their attitudes to the police force. Individual depth interviews can be used to check attitudes expressed outside a group situation or to explore detailed individual behaviour. Depth interviews and group discussions are often seen as complementary in qualitative research.

Market research in the UK (especially the qualitative variety) consistently ignores the existence of about 5 per cent of the population. In my own experience, if you set up a typical group discussion the chances of seeing a black face among the white ones is pretty remote.

One can speculate on the reasons for this. Recruiters often aim for a degree of uniformity within a group which they fear would be compromised by including a black person. They know that if a group they have recruited 'goes well', according to the moderator, they are more likely to be asked for their services again. Equally, they might, for a host of reasons, feel unwilling to approach a black person for recruitment into a group. A very large West Indian said to me the other day, 'If I was a white interviewer and had to rely on the media for my knowledge of black people, there's no way I'd ever approach someone like me with a clipboard and a questionnaire.' Ignorance, fear and prejudice go hand in hand. There is a gulf between black and white in this country which means that blacks are, in effect, an invisible minority as far as market research is concerned. Yet this population numbers some 2½–4 million, depending on your source of statistics and how you interpret them.

'Blacks' and 'whites'

The terms 'black' and 'white' tend to be used loosely and glibly. To what extent can they – and should they – be employed to distinguish between the cumbersomely labelled 'ethnic minorities' and the rest?

The great majority of the ethnic minority population of the UK are from what is commonly called the 'New Commonwealth, plus Pakistan'. This is roughly equivalent to the present Commonwealth, leaving out Australia, New Zealand and Canada. (The UK attracts a lot of visitors, but not many permanent immigrants from these 'Old Commonwealth' countries.) These ethnic groups in the descending order of their numerical importance are: India; Caribbean (plus Guyana); Pakistan; Mediterranean (Cyprus, Malta); East Africa (Kenya, Tanzania, Uganda, including many East African Indians); Far East (Hong Kong, Singapore, Malaysia); Bangladesh (formerly part of Pakistan). There are a great many other countries each contributing relatively small numbers to the total ethnic community – Sri Lanka, Southern Africa, West Africa, etc.

Because of the way census figures are gathered this is only a rough and ready guide, and I would not want to start putting numbers against any of these groups. (People from ethnic minorities are defined as persons in households of which the head was born in the given country. It involves an overcount arising from the inclusion of, for example, white 'refugees' from India and East Africa, and an undercount arising from the exclusion of West Indian households with a UK-born head of household.)

So far, in all the ethnic minority projects we have been involved in, the Mediterranean population has been excluded on the basis that they are more assimilated, less culturally different, or suffer fewer problems of adaptation. Some other numerically less important groups have also been excluded. For these reasons 'ethnic minorities' has come to mean, for our research purposes, three very broad and distinctive groups: West Indians; people from the Indian sub-continent (including via East Africa); and Chinese.

Mixing and matching

To what extent do these groups have to be sub-divided? We have found that it is generally possible to mix West Indians from different islands (and from Guyana). Jamaicans are by far the most numerous and most typical West Indian group discussions would include some Jamaicans and people from several other islands. Although Jamaica tends to be seen as a 'big brother' (sometimes a big bad brother) in the Caribbean, this does not have an undesirable effect on West Indian groups recruited in the UK. One needs to be much more discriminating with communities from the Indian sub-continent. There are at least three important interacting variables to consider: locality, religion and language. Probably the most important variable is religion: there is a profound difference between Hindus and Muslims in terms of behaviour, attitudes, diet, customs and social restriction. But this is not the only religious divide: one would not normally want to mix Hindus and Sikhs, for example. In terms of religion the two are related, but politically they are currently at odds in the Punjab.

Similarly, it cannot be assumed that a group of 'Hindus' will have much to say to each other: half could speak Hindi, the other half Gujarati. And people from the same country (for example, Bangladesh), sharing the same religion, will not necessarily share the same spoken language.

'Black' and 'white' (again!)

Let us return to the sometimes contentious terms 'black' and 'white'. We have found these two adjectives to be the clearest and most useful ones when setting up, conducting and reporting on ethnic minority research involving West Indians, Asians and Chinese. A moment's thought will convince you that terms such as 'English', 'British', 'immigrants' or 'ethnics' are not very satisfactory for distinguishing at the simplest level between these different groups.

We were not surprised to find that West Indians have no objection to being referred to collectively as 'blacks', but we did not expect Indians or Chinese to welcome being categorized in this way. To our surprise we found that generally they had no objections. While the skin colour of Indians or Chinese is patently not black, we found that many of our respondents felt that politically and socially they were 'black', in that they suffered from the same patterns of prejudice from the white community. For qualitative research purposes we usually adopt simple definitions for 'black' and 'white'.

Black

Born in the country in question, or both parents born there. This means that West Indians who have never seen the Caribbean could be included in a sample of young West Indians.

White

Born in the UK of parents of UK descent.

Why ethnic research?

So far I have mentioned some reasons for *not* including ethnic minorities in market research, and have hinted at some of the difficulties of defining terms. The more positive reasons for addressing ethnic minority groups (the list is *not* in any particular order) are: numbers – and growth; special products; special target groups for advertising; good relations.

Numbers

As I have already mentioned, ethnic minorities account for 5 per cent plus of the UK population. There are signs that a few advertisers are at least beginning to realize that it is foolish to ignore several million consumers. Parts of this population – notably the Bangladeshis – are growing much faster than the population as a whole, a fact which is made much of by certain politicians. I would make the point, however, that figures for population growth are notoriously difficult to interpret and project. One has to consider differences in the average age of the population, for example, which are related to how long ago the main influx was: relatively recently, in the case of the Bangladeshis. Another factor is the education gap between different communities (itself a rapidly changing statistic) which is reflected in the use – or non-use – of modern contraceptive techniques.

Products

Certain products have an almost exclusively ethnic market, particularly among foods. Examples are Nutrament (and variants) in the West Indian community, as well as a wide range of exotic fruits and vegetables, panir and khoya in the Indian/Pakistani communities, bean curd in the Chinese community. The dairy products I have mentioned have been up to now largely ignored by the major UK-based manufacturers.

An example of a very important food with a special ethnic aspect is canned meat targeted at the Muslim community. All meat – fresh, canned or otherwise processed – consumed by Muslims has to conform to the religious laws pertaining to the kind of animal and the way in which it is slaughtered. It is thus essential that labelling should convey the appropriate information clearly and authoritatively. For a UK packer, careful ethnic research is the only way of establishing that his labelling meets these requirements.

Advertising target groups

It is a regrettable fact that the ethnic minorities (as a whole, not separately) are over-represented in the prison population but under-represented in the police force. Advertising has recently been produced aimed specifically at ethnic minorities, even to the extent of publishing it in a number of ethnic languages – Gujarati, Urdu, Bengali, Punjabi and Hindi.

Good relations

Any sensible advertiser should consider, if a black person is to appear in his advertising, how black people will react to it. It can be extremely difficult and downright foolhardy for a white person to speculate on this from behind a desk. Partly because black people appear so rarely in advertising, blacks often show extreme sensitivity to how they are depicted. They are likely to infer messages, intentions, prejudices and so on which in fact had never occurred to the advertiser or the agency.

Qualitative research on such advertising represents at the very least an insurance premium for the advertiser. Its value increases as the voice of ethnic minorities becomes stronger and more confident.

Case 6: Earthmovers

The Hertz Corporation has been market leader in construction equipment rental in North America for many years. Whereas in its other fields Hertz operates on an international basis, with equipment rental it was active only in the US. When, therefore, Hertz decided to expand its rental operation, this had to mean going international and Europe was the natural target.

Hertz, of course, had much going for it. Its equipment rental operation in the US had given it vast experience of this sector; its financial resources were impressive and so far as automotive rental was concerned it already had a world-wide network. What it lacked was knowledge and experience of the construction equipment market in Europe and for this it turned to The Corporate Intelligence Group.

At least Hertz appreciated from the start that European countries would have to be appraised individually. Many American organizations which are not already trading on this side of the Atlantic think of Europe as one single, unified market. In reality, of course, 1992 is a long way away; even then national characteristics and environmental factors will still mean that marketing strategy has to be planned on a national rather than multinational basis.

This was certainly true of the equipment rental sector. All countries are involved in construction and construction activity needs construction equipment, the market for which is world-wide. Most major suppliers now have their equipment available in all the developed countries. But if the market for construction equipment has become truly world-wide in scope, the same cannot be said of the concept of equipment rental.

In the UK the equipment rental companies have been part of the infrastructure for years. Previous research by the Corporate Intelligence Group had established that the plant hire industry consists of 5,000 companies; employs 50,000 persons; has an annual turnover of £1 billion; owns plant and equipment valued at £1.3 billion.

It would have been easy to assume that the infrastructure would exist – to a greater or lesser extent – in the mainland European countries. The Corporate Intelligence Group, because of the activities of its specialist Off Highway Research Division, knew that this was not the case and right from the start had a good idea of what to expect.

At the other end of the scale, for example, Italy has no formally organized plant hire operation whatsoever. In the middle of the spectrum come countries like France where the concept is known, but only applied in some geographic areas and then in a piecemeal and fragmented way. This is not to say that the absence of an established rental industry *in itself* said anything about the prospects for Hertz in the country concerned. In such areas the key issue was then whether the industry climate was right for the introduction of the concept. Was there a danger that Hertz would go in, open up and educate the market only for others to move in close behind and reap the benefits of Hertz's investment? Hertz needed The Consultants to appraise their prospects in each of the European countries and, where those prospects looked encouraging, to advise The Corporation on the best means of entering that market. That meant the obvious choice between a joint venture with an existing operator; the acquisition of an existing and suitable player; or a 'green fields' operation with Hertz making the running on their own. The Corporate Intelligence Group knew that the choice was in reality more complex than that, since with either acquisition or joint venture the target company could be already in the rental business or it could be in a related sector: for example, as an equipment distributor. The less well developed the rental concept, the more likely it was that the latter would be the case.

If Hertz wanted the research to answer the same questions in all countries, the Corporate Intelligence Group knew that the methodology would have to vary from country to country, being determined by existing practices and attitudes. Each country had to be tackled in its own right, with a study tailor-made to local conditions. Besides measuring and appraising the current and/or potential market for equipment rental in each country, Hertz needed advice on:

(a) what equipment to offer in each country they entered. Their initial list was long and the Corporation needed to know if all the equipment proposed was appropriate. Guidance was wanted also on what make(s) to offer within each of the product categories;

(b) the target companies to be considered for acquisition or joint venture: this meant not only identifying but profiling target companies.

However, Hertz were far-sighted enough to allow the Corporate Intelligence Group to reveal their name and interest during fieldwork. It was realized that their image could have a significant effect on subsequent market performance and company reaction. This indeed made The Consultants' life much easier. There is often much to be gained in real terms for clients having their identity revealed in such studies, albeit on a selective basis.

The Corporate Intelligence Group's method of working is ideally suited to this kind of study. All such enquiries are run from its London office, with multilingual consultants going out from London to conduct fieldwork in the countries concerned. Work is never sub-contracted to independent and autonomous local associates or affiliates. The additional costs involved, relating almost entirely to travel and subsistence, are more than offset by the improved quality of information obtained: the researchers can be better briefed in terms of industry and company information, particularly in this case where The Consultants already maintained an extensive computerized database on the industry; and the approach is much more systematic, since it is centrally planned and controlled.

The international comparisons are much more thorough and meaningful when the full research team can sit down and discuss their findings with the project director. Hertz were well aware that even a Corporation of their size could not hope to move into several countries simultaneously. There was a limit as to what could be handled at any point in time and the Corporation was therefore happy to work out the batting order with The Consultants.

So far the research has been carried out in five countries: Great Britain, France, West Germany, Italy and Spain. Interviews have been carried out with top management in some forty companies in each country. The 'tailor-made' approach was proved to be totally justified, since the variation by country was considerable.

As already noted, the industry in Great Britain is highly developed and, in its search for new growth areas, has diversified into new products. It has followed the construction industry's move into repair, maintenance and refurbishment and has been offering a range of powered access platforms, mini excavators and rough terrain forklift excavators and rough terrain forklift trucks. These machines, along with the well-established backhoe loaders, site dumpers, compressors and compaction equipment, now form the basis of the most successful plant hire fleets.

The most topical current growth hire market is in small tool hire and the do-it-yourself (DIY) business. Large national and regional plant hire groups with local chainstores, contractors and even owner-operators are branching out into opening up hire shops, offering anything from small tools to mini excavators. In these circumstances not surprisingly it was found that acquisition was the best route to take and there was no shortage of potential targets.

In Germany, on the other hand, the rental business does not really exist. Moreover, little interest was shown in the concept of renting; indeed, the Germans have been as enthusiastic in adopting plant rental as they have been in adopting credit in consumer markets. The market for construction equipment may be high, but construction companies are only interested in buying. This being so, market entry through acquisition or joint venture was not applicable. If Hertz's wish was to enter the market, it could only have been through a 'green fields' operation, but only if Hertz believed they could change attitudes to and interest in renting. The Corporate Intelligence Group's recommendation had to be to stay out of West Germany. The recommendation was accepted. The position varied between these extremes in the other countries.

In Spain, for example, plant hire had become established in five product areas: sectors such as welding and gensets, mobile compressors, pumps and some compaction equipment. With other products no impact had been made. Moreover, hire was invariably with operator (usually this meant owner/operator) and in many ways was more akin to sub-contracting than the form of non-operator hire we are so familiar with in this country. Furthermore, where hire was becoming established, it was attracting many small operators and the market was becoming fiercely competitive with very low rates. The prospects for Hertz were limited and confined to particular market segments.

In Italy there was no existing plant hire market and structurally, therefore, Italy was in the same position as Germany. But in Italy there is a large and expanding construction and building industry, currently relying on ownership of plant but ready, particularly in such areas as repair, maintenance and refurbishment work, to turn to plant hire instead. The prospects were far better for plant hire, particularly in certain large industrial areas where the volume of potential business was high. Moreover, it was possible for The Consultants to identify dealer networks open to acquisition which could then provide the framework for a plant hire operation.

Hertz found detailed results of these studies invaluable, allowing them to move rapidly in entering these markets. The emphasis throughout was on actionable recommendations, with help from The Consultants in implementing those recommendations. It was not simply about measuring market size and attitudes to plant hire; it was about identifying target companies and making the necessary introductions; about evaluating various types of equipment; about identifying the best locations. To date Hertz have accepted the Corporate Intelligence Group's recommendations on Italy and Germany, have acted on the recommendation for the UK and are doing so currently in France, and will then move to Spain. The Consultants could not ask for more.

Case 7: Evaluating direct selling effectiveness

A company sold a range of products into the home through a network of part-time agents, working on a commission-only basis. The products had a broad range of appeal, and typically in a customer household, several family members would make purchases. Accounts could be settled in full on receipt of the goods, or by ten weekly instalments. Interest was applied to instalment payments. About a quarter of customers paid by instalments. The company approached a market research agency with the following problem:

There was considerable variation in the amount of business achieved by agents. High achieving agents reached sales levels many times those of the low achievers. Not only this, but low achieving agents tended to sell only at the peak season, and to be inactive for the rest of the year, while high-achievers continued to sell throughout the year although they, too, show a seasonal peak in their sales.

Research was required to explain the differences and to identify ways in which low-achieving agents could be motivated to increase their sales volume.

The company had available a considerable amount of detailed information about its agents – length of time with the company, number of customers, value and frequency of order, geographical location, etc. – which had already been analysed in detail. Previous surveys had established the demographic profiles of agents analysed by level of sales; high and low achieving agents were not differentiated on demographic grounds. Consequently, a qualitative investigation was proposed, and accordingly a number of group discussions were conducted. The company supplied lists of agents from which the research agency was able to locate clusters of agents living near enough to each other to be able to meet together at a central location – a domestic living-room – where the group discussion could take place in relaxed, informal surroundings.

High achieving agents and low achievers were recruited into separate groups, and there were further splits between recent and long-established agents, and between those from the BC1 social grades and those from the C2D grades. Groups were convened at three different locations around the UK to give a broad national coverage.

To allocate one group to each cell in each region would have demanded twenty-four groups in total. It was felt that such a large number was unnecessary and, of course, extremely expensive. A partial design was adopted, whereby inferences could be drawn about the influence of region, social grade and length of time as an agent on the level of sales achieved, and yet only twelve group discussions were required.

The research achieved its prime objective of explaining the difference in performance among agents. It was discovered that high achieving agents shared a perception of themselves as engaged in self-employed work. This being the case, they placed importance on regular contact with their customers and on the pursuit of new customers. Since they were looking for a regular income from their selling activities, they were at pains to actively encourage their customers to buy.

Low achieving agents, by contrast, saw themselves as engaged in essentially social activity. To them, the commission they received was useful – it helped to fund their own purchases – but secondary to the socializing from which the sales arose. Thus, they tended to restrict their selling to friends, neighbours and workmates. Moreover, unless they or a family member wished to order something, they were unlikely to seek out sales from others. It was clear from the research that little or nothing could be done that would be cost-effective to motivate low achievers to generate a higher rate of sale. They were content with the level of earnings they achieved and had no desire to increase their effort, and thus dilute the social content of their activity.

As a consequence of the research, the company concentrated on motivating high achievers to expand their activities still more, while at the same time adopting procedures which required the low achievers to come up to a minimum level acceptable to the company or drop out. This had the effect that gradually the range of sales levels narrowed, and the mean value of sales per agent increased.

Case 8: Evaluating sports sponsorship

Dow is one of the largest chemical and plastics producers in the world. Dow, like its competitors, has had to become more involved in corporate and brand advertising and, more recently, in sponsorship. In 1986 Dow decided to sponsor a ladies' tennis tournament that had been held in Edgbaston, Birmingham for a number of years. Dow invited DVL Smith & Associates, an independent business research agency, to evaluate the effectiveness of its sponsorship of the Dow Classic and to help the company decide whether or not to continue with the sponsorship.

The starting-point for the research was a series of depth interviews with key senior Dow managers drawn from general management, marketing and public relations, aimed at building up a picture of the company's expectations of the event. DVL Smith & Associates worked on the basis that if the research was to have any credibility then the criteria against which the sponsorship would be evaluated must be fully endorsed by Dow's senior management. We took the view that without consensus support for the evaluation criteria, the study would be doomed; individuals could dissent from the research conclusions on the grounds that they thought the sponsorship was trying to achieve different goals from the ones we were measuring. It was agreed that the main criteria to be taken into account should include the extent to which the event provided an appropriate forum for entertaining Dow's business customers (and their partners); generated awareness of the Dow name; built visibility of Dow in industrial markets; enhanced Dow's image in the marketplace; built morale among Dow employees; and provided a showcase around which Dow could recruit graduate staff. In addition it was agreed that in assessing the effectiveness of the Dow Classic, the way in which sponsorship works in a cumulative way over time would be taken into account. It was also acknowledged that sponsorship rarely works as an aware- ness- and image-building vehicle on its own; thus the assessment of awareness and image would need to be made in the context of the wider package of Dow's marketing and communications initiatives.

The research programme, designed to evaluate the extent to which the Dow Classic was meeting the objectives that had been set for the event, was an eclectic one. First, DVL Smith & Associates conducted a programme of desk research. We gathered around us all there was to know about sports, and particularly tennis, sponsorship. Secondly, we had an opportunity of evaluating the 1988 Dow Classic, the last event before Dow's option for sponsorship of the event came up for renewal. A research team from DVL Smith & Associates attended all seven days of the event, taking photographs and noting aspects of the tournament that might be improved in the future. In addition, DVL Smith & Associates attended other sponsored events in order to provide a benchmark against which to evaluate the standard of the Dow event, and in particular its corporate hospitality. Throughout the tournament checks were made on national and local TV and radio coverage of the Dow Classic. We also assessed the coverage the event was getting via the Superchannel satellite network.

The research programme included interviews with a total of forty customers, plus twenty partners of customers, who attended the Dow Classic as guests of Dow. A proportion of these interviews were conducted at the event itself, with the remainder taking place three weeks after the event. We also conducted a range of telephone interviews with individuals who were invited but were unable to attend the event. We conducted twenty-one interviews with Dow employees, and a total of 101 interviews with visitors to the Dow

Classic, over five of the seven days of the tournament. Finally, six interviews were conducted with specialists in the field of tennis and sponsorship, promotion and business entertainment. This phase of research included conducting interviews with press representatives attending the Dow Classic.

The research study showed that tennis, as a popular sport with an upmarket image, was very much compatible with Dow's image. The only slight limitation was that certain individuals found women's tennis less dynamic than men's. While it was established that other sports such as golf, cricket and rugby also seemed to fit the Dow image, there was no evidence to suggest that they would prove more effective than tennis. The research also established that the idea of combining business entertainment, Dow's primary objective, with the secondary objective of awareness and image building, seemed to work well. Attendance at a Dow organized event did not expose Dow's customers to competitors and we established that attendance at such an event, when professionally executed, made customers feel important. The event conveyed a sense of solidarity; the Dow Classic was a concrete manifestation of Dow's corporate identity. We further demonstrated that the event provided a fillip for Dow employees who were involved. It would have been impossible to achieve all of the above via alternative business entertainment, and perhaps even through an alternative sponsorship format. The research also went on to identify specifically the way in which the event *works* in terms of business entertainment. But the event did not get a completely clean bill of health.

The research established that the future of the Dow Classic depended on Dow being able to attract more top name players than had been the case in the past. Secondly, the research showed that more could be done to promote the Dow name at the event. One particular confusion was the rather muddled approach to the presentation of *both* the corporate Dow logo and individual branded products at the event. Thirdly, the research unearthed certain weaknesses in the way business customers attending the event were targeted: to justify the investment it was important that the key decision takers from major customer companies attended. Furthermore, at a tactical level the research identified a long list of specific improvements that could be made to the event, including ensuring that the Dow logo appeared on the scoreboard.

Dow accepted the findings of the research and a decision was taken to extend Dow's sponsorship of the Dow Classic. Also, importantly, steps were taken to enhance the status of the event, culminating in Martina Navratilova becoming the Dow Classic ladies' champion in

1989. In addition, Dow has tightened up its procedures for targeting business customers, and has also introduced a wide range of improvements in order to sharpen the presentation of the Dow image at the event. At one point there was a danger that Dow could pull out of the event, but thanks to a formal and systematic programme of research it was possible to identify the exact way in which the Dow Classic was working, thereby allowing sensible strategic decisions to be made about its longer term future.

Index

Index

Statistical Package for the Social Sciences
  (SPSS), 111–12
statistical symbols, 27–8
synetics, 46

tachistoscope, 56
Target Group Index (TGI), 60, 80
Technical Help to Exporters (*see* British
  Standards Institution)
telephone directories, bias in samples, 35
telephone enquiries, 35–6

telephone surveys in industrial marketing
  research, 66
television advertising research, 58
test marketing, 54–5
thematic apperception test, 45
trade directories (*see* desk research)

unobtrusive measures, 31

word association test, 45